T0317706

RESISTING AI

"Rethinks AI from the ground up. It is not corporate 'ethics' that AI needs, but far-reaching politics, reworking AI not as a 'revolutionary technology' but as a technology for revolution."
Matthew Fuller, Goldsmiths, University of London

"With analytical and moral clarity, McQuillan makes the case for recognising the radical politics of AI and meeting its goose step march head-on."
Jathan Sadowski, Monash University

RESISTING AI

An Anti-fascist Approach to
Artificial Intelligence

Dan McQuillan

BRISTOL
UNIVERSITY
PRESS

First published in Great Britain in 2022 by

Bristol University Press
University of Bristol
1-9 Old Park Hill
Bristol
BS2 8BB
UK
t: +44 (0)117 374 6645
e: bup-info@bristol.ac.uk

Details of international sales and distribution partners are available at
bristoluniversitypress.co.uk

British Library Cataloguing in Publication Data
A catalogue record for this book is available from the British Library

ISBN 978-1-5292-1349-2 hardcover
ISBN 978-1-5292-1350-8 paperback
ISBN 978-1-5292-1351-5 ePub
ISBN 978-1-5292-1352-2 ePdf

Cover design by Nicky Borowiec
Front cover image: Adobe Stock/ Dmitry 217187220

Printed and bound by CPI Group (UK) Ltd, Croydon, CR0 4YY

For Njomëza, Khayam & Lira

Contents

Acknowledgements

I want to thank the editorial team at Bristol University Press, in particular Paul Stevens who invited me to write the book. My gratitude goes to the small band of brave readers who reviewed early versions of the text: Harry Browne, Graeme Tiffany, Tom Wakeford, Susan Kelly, Sanela Jahic, Michael Castelle, Mark Simpkins, James Burton and Giacomo Antonelli. With this book, as with all my writing, I rely on the clear-sightedness of my good friend and comrade, Cliff Ashcroft. Special thanks are due to my wife, Njömeza, who always encouraged me to write a book and then had the patience to put up with me when I finally did. I will always be grateful to my parents, Bill & Imelda, for their enduring guidance and care.

Introduction

What is AI

This book is about how and why we should resist the introduction of artificial intelligence, or AI. It hopes to persuade the reader that resistance is what is needed, by showing how AI represents a technological shift in the framework of society that will amplify austerity while enabling authoritarian politics. However, despite the presentation of the varieties of AI harmfulness in the first part of the book, it is intended as an ultimately optimistic text, one that holds out the possibility of a radically transformative approach to AI that aligns with wider values of care and the common good. But before we get into discussing these developments, let alone what part we can play in them, we need to clarify what we mean by AI itself.

The book is concerned with actual AI as it operates in the world, not with the grandiose rhetoric or sci-fi storylines that obscure it. AI is, on a basic level, a set of specific computational operations, and Chapter 1 sets out to demystify these operations by bringing them out from behind the veil of technical obfuscation. However, AI is always more than a set of machine learning methods. When we're thinking about the actuality of AI, we can't separate the calculations in the code from the social context of its application. AI is never separate from the assembly of institutional arrangements that need to be in place for it to make an impact in society. Likewise, these institutions are immersed in wider frameworks of understanding that carry implicit and explicit assumptions about how the world is to be differentiated and valued. AI, as it is talked about in this book, is this layered and interdependent arrangement of technology, institutions and ideology. The general term we will use for this arrangement is 'apparatus'.

Most of this book uses deep learning as its technical reference point because deep learning is the dominant form of AI at the time of writing. It's important to refer to the actual technology because one of the themes of this text is that political impacts arise from resonances between concrete technical characteristics and the surrounding social and political conditions. Understanding AI means understanding its specific computational operations and everything that is being carried along by them; the history that AI has absorbed, the world in which it is emerging, and the futures that it calls forth. Some of what may seem, at the start, like nerdish technical detail will turn out to have significant political implications.

Having said that, the analysis presented here is not limited to deep learning. On the one hand, as the intent of the text is to interrupt the most dangerous tendencies incipient in AI before they come to pass, some of the case studies are not applications of AI as such but of precursor algorithmic systems; that is, algorithms that play some role in automated decision making but which are not themselves forms of machine learning. On the other hand, the broader thrust of the argument addresses not only deep learning, and its close cousins like reinforcement learning, but any subsequent computational system that offers a form of statistical optimization as a solution to social problems. As we'll see in more detail as we go through the book, any AI-like system will act as a condenser for existing forms of structural and cultural violence.

AI, as we know it, is a kind of computing, but it's also a form of knowledge production, a paradigm for social organization and a political project. While it might be interesting in another context to ask philosophical questions about the meaning of intelligence and whether it can ever be artificial, that's not the concern of this book, which instead sets out to ask what part AI plays in history as we are living it. Whatever else AI is, it is not neutral, and neither can we be. AI is political because it acts in the world in ways that affect the distribution of power, and its political tendencies are revealed in the ways that it sets up boundaries and separations. The apparatus of AI forms feedback loops with the rest of society: it's "a structured structure that becomes a structuring structure" (Bourdieu, 1980, cited in

Castelle, 2018). The focus here is on the ways that AI will alter the landscapes of our lives.

Resisting AI

The public narrative around AI has created high expectations. In the last few years AI seems to have accelerated from movie trope to material reality, with our cities about to be filled with self-driving cars and our health conditions diagnosed earlier and more accurately by apps. AI is being heralded as a potential solution to societal ills from child protection to climate change. On the other hand, this very acceleration has stirred up apocalyptic fears, from predictions by business pundits that AI will take all our jobs to the vision of AI as a dystopian superior intelligence. The superintelligent AI apocalypse is taken sufficiently seriously to occupy the full attention of both philosophers (Bostrom, 2014) and leading computer scientists in the field (Russell, 2020).

This book agrees that AI is important but not for any of the reasons given above. The theme explored throughout the text is that AI is a political technology in its material existence and in its effects. The concrete operations of AI are completely entangled with the social matrix around them, and the book argues that the consequences are politically reactionary. The net effect of applied AI, it is claimed, is to amplify existing inequalities and injustices, deepening existing divisions on the way to full-on algorithmic authoritarianism. In the light of these consequences, which are justified more fully in the following chapters, the book is titled after the stance it hopes to encourage, namely that of 'resisting AI'.

Rather than focusing on what might happen if AI developed superintelligence, we look in Chapter 1 at the narrower reality of what AI technologies actually do; how their algorithms work, where the data comes from, and what social patterns feed in and out of these computational operations. The chapter digs into deep learning to reveal both its clever statistical manipulations and the gulf between this and anything we'd acknowledge as human-like intelligence. More importantly, it traces how the specific data transformations of deep learning shape its likely social effects. The chapter also looks at the hidden labour relations without which deep learning would not exist, and at the substrate of circuits and servers that require vast systems of cooling and energy supply.

Chapter 2 makes it clear that AI, as it actually exists, is a fragile technology, which should face fundamental questions about its unexpected failure modes, its lack of explainability and its amplification of unwelcome cultural patterns. It explores the way AI's brittleness overwhelmingly causes harm to people who are already marginalized, and sets out the reasons why current remedies, from ethical principles to legal regulation, and from technical fixes to the human-in-the-loop, have little traction on constraining these harms. It highlights the way AI is sold as a solution to social problems, when what it is really doing is applying algorithmic morality judgements to target groups while obscuring the structural drivers of the very problems it is supposedly solving.

It would be troubling enough if AI was a technology being tested in the lab or applied in a few pioneering startups, but it already has huge institutional and cultural momentum. As we see in Chapter 3, AI derives a lot of its authority from its association with methods of scientific analysis, especially abstraction and reduction, an association which also fuels the hubris of some of its practitioners. The roll out of AI across swathes of industry doesn't so much lead to a loss of jobs as to an amplification of casualized and precarious work. Rather than being an apocalyptic technology, AI is more aptly characterized as a form of supercharged bureaucracy that ramps up everyday cruelties, such as those in our systems of welfare. In general, according to Chapter 3, AI doesn't lead to a new dystopia ruled over by machines but an intensification of existing misery through speculative tendencies that echo those of finance capital. These tendencies are given a particular cutting edge by the way AI operates with and through race. AI is a form of computation that inherits concepts developed under colonialism and reproduces them as a form of race science. This is the payload of real AI under the status quo.

What we should also be examining, given the current state of global financial, epidemiological and ecological conditions, are the tendencies enabled by AI in times of crisis, and this is the focus of Chapter 4. The latest wave of AI has come to prominence in the period following the 2008 financial crash, and its ability to optimize rationing at scale readily fits in with austerity policies based on scarcity. Chapter 4 focuses on the way AI enables the kinds of exclusions that appeal all too easily to carceral states and security regimes. The polarization of outcomes under COVID-19, with their echoes of eugenics, flags up the way a crisis can rationalize the disposability of some for the good of the remainder, and we should be attentive to the ways algorithmic ranking can play a part in that.

Chapter 4 is a call to action regarding the potential of AI under crisis and the way the pseudo-rational ideology of artificial intelligence, with its racist and supremacist undertones, makes it an attractive prospect for the already existing authoritarian and fascist tendencies in political movements around the world. Given this, a shift to resisting AI is not only necessary but urgent. As we look forward with trepidation to the consequences of the climate crisis, with the likelihood that privilege will be defended, responsibility deflected and the vulnerable sacrificed, our priority for advanced technologies like AI should be to ask not only how they can be prevented from intensifying harm but how we can reassert the primacy of the common good.

Anti-fascist approach

At this point, we need to clarify why we're also talking about an anti-fascist approach to AI. In part, it's because fascism never really went away, something that's clearer every day with the rise of fascist-influenced political parties in so many countries. Given the real existing threat of fascist and authoritarian politics, we should be especially wary of any emerging technology of control that might end up being deployed by such regimes. But the main reasons for having an anti-fascist approach to AI run deeper into the nature of the technology itself and its approach to the world. It's not just about the possibility of AI being used by authoritarian regimes but about the resonances between AI's operations and the underlying conditions that give rise to those regimes. In particular, it's about the resonances between AI and the emergence of fascistic solutions to social problems.

To be clear, this book doesn't claim some deterministic link between AI and fascism: it's not saying that AI is fascist. However, what brings an instance of fascism into play as a historical force is a confluence of various factors, and it's in relation to these precursor currents that the character of AI becomes especially relevant. The conditions that need to be present for fascism to become a serious force are both ideological and opportunistic; the ideas have to be present but so do the particular kinds of crises that cause those ideas to look like a solution (Malm and The Zetkin Collective, 2021). AI's potential contribution is as a vector for normalizing specific kinds of responses to social instabilities.

Being alert to this possibility means having some idea about fascist ideology and the conditions under which it tends to thrive. In terms of ideology, we can refer to a widely used, if somewhat condensed, summary of fascism that describes it as 'palingenetic ultranationalism' (Griffin, 1993). These two words distill the ideology into features that are constant over time, and helps us to avoid getting diverted into looking for exact repeats of fascist rhetoric from the 1930s. The palingenetic bit simply means national rebirth; that the nation needs to be reborn from some kind of current decadence and reclaim its glorious past, a process which will inevitably be violent. The term ultranationalism indicates that we're not talking about a nation defined by citizenship but by organic membership of an ethnic community. Hence, with AI, we should be watchful for functionality that contributes to violent separations of 'us and them', especially those that seem to essentialize differences.

In terms of the political and social conditions, what is required to trigger a turn to fascism is a deep social crisis of some kind. The extremist ideas of fascism only start to have mass appeal when there's a sense of existential risk. For a crisis to be 'fascism-inducing' or 'fascism-producing' (Eley, 2016, cited in Malm and The Zetkin Collective, 2021) it has to appear to be beyond the capacity of traditional systems to solve. But this is only one side of the equation; the other is the decision of the dominant social class to invoke fascistic forces as a way to preserve their existing power. Historical fascisms have never actually come about through revolution but by the decision of the existing elites that they needed it as a prop for a collapsing hegemony

(Paxton, 2005). So, as far as AI is concerned, we need to be aware of both dynamics: the forms of crisis under which AI emerges and for which it is seen as a potential solution, and the aspirations of elites to use AI as a way to maintain existing political and cultural privilege.

So, the starting point for an anti-fascist approach to AI is an alertness to its operation as a technology of division, to its promotion as a solution for social crisis, and to its use to prop up power and privilege. The argument is not that the only problem with AI is the potential to enable fascistic or authoritarian politics; there are many immediately harmful aspects of AI, as we shall explore in the coming chapters. But it is warning of fascism as a political possibility that shouldn't be ignored, and an assertion that any tendency to facilitate a shift in that direction should help to shape our response to AI as a whole. An anti-fascist approach is not simply one that opposes fascist tendencies but one that actively works towards structural alternatives to the conditions that give rise to the possibility of fascism in the first place.

In effect, AI acts as a kind of 'metapolitics', a term which some elements of the modern far right use for the process of shifting what's politically acceptable by shifting the culture that's upstream of it. Our concern with AI is not that it is fascist per se but that, because of its core operations, it lends itself to 'fascization', or solutions operating in the direction of fascism, and it is these that we need to be alert for as we go through the book. Likewise, having an anti-fascist approach to AI means being alert to these tendencies before they can bear fruit; it means countering any sign of such metapolitics by substituting in its place a project for a better society.

From machine learning to mutual aid

Having laid out, in Chapters 1 to 4, the reactionary politics of AI and the inability of reformist regulation to restrain it, we use Chapter 5 to scope out an alternative approach. AI's exclusions have roots going all the way down through our social structures and our ways of knowing. Fortunately, we don't have to invent a remedy for this from scratch because there are already perspectives and practices that will help us to overcome these exclusions. In Chapter 5 we start with feminist standpoint theory, which undermines the absolutist form of scientific authority that AI tries to cloak itself with. Feminist and decolonial critiques of science can help change AI's approach to generating knowledge in ways that prioritize marginalized perspectives.

One of the fundamental positions set out in Chapter 5 is that boundaries are always constructed and what matters most is the forms of relationality that are at work in constructing those boundaries. One of the most toxic tendencies of socially applied AI is to naturalize and essentialize structural differences as part of an 'us and them' politics of inequality. Looking at AI from this different perspective allows us to understand it as an apparatus that helps produce aspects of the world through the exclusions it sets up, and suggests ways that we can interrupt this through horizontal forms of intervention. Chapter 5 articulates a collective approach to problem solving so as to open up new possibilities beyond the predictions of AI, in particular by shifting the focus from statistical inference to mutual care.

Of course, it's all very well having an alternative ethics and epistemology but what we really need are ways to turn these into tactics. Chapter 6 asks what practices can enact an alternative AI, and what forms of organization we require. The chapter proposes that the social tactic that goes with an ethics of care is mutual aid, and that the action–oriented commitment accompanying it is solidarity. It argues that mutual aid and solidarity are the basis for opposing precarity and overturning AI-driven states of exception. It looks at the stirrings of dissent within the AI industry itself among workers who already see how things are going wrong, and suggests self-organized worker's councils as a way to generalize a transformation from within. It extends this approach beyond the workplace through the model of the people's council as a form of constituent counter-power, one that assembles workers and communities into social movements capable of interrupting AI and pushing for transformative change.

Understanding AI not as some futuristic tech that has appeared in the present, but as a product of historical social processes, allows us to learn lessons from history about how best to deal with it. In the same way that Chapter 5 uses critiques from the history of science to challenge AI's claims to authority, the proposals for worker's and people's councils in Chapter 6 draw from a long historical pedigree of political struggle against injustice and authoritarianism. One of the historical struggles against top-down technological transformation that has particular lessons for AI is Luddism. Chapter 6 looks at the similarities between Luddite times and the present day, in relation to the combination of social crisis and new forms of automation, and recovers from Luddism a sense of militancy and a commitment to the common good.

Overall, it is argued in Chapter 7, these radical perspectives can be gathered under the rubric of an anti-fascist approach to AI. This is partly about the early recognition of the threat posed by AI and having the determination to tackle it directly, but it goes beyond refusal to become a reorientation towards alternatives. Acknowledging that the roots of the problem lie in the status quo means actively pushing for a better world, one in which, by refusing computational exclusions and states of exception, we can centre the practices of mutual care. Resisting AI is significantly about restructuring the conditions that give rise to AI.

Chapter 7 draws the book to a close by setting out some sustainable directions for our technical apparatuses. It draws on historical and contemporary movements, like socially useful production and solidarity economies, to illustrate the wider idea of structural renewal and its relevance to the question of AI. Of particular importance here are the ideas of the commons and commonality, both in terms of the desirability that our apparatuses should contribute to the common good, and in terms of the specific role that 'commoning' can play in the transformation of techno-social systems. *Resisting AI* helps to illuminate a way forward for tech under the conditions of the coming global crisis.

1

Operations of AI

This chapter takes a look at the operations of AI, that is, at the kind of computation that currently carries the title of 'artificial intelligence'. It looks in turn at machine learning, at deep learning and at the infrastructure that supports them. One reason to have a close look at the actual operations of AI is to debunk the association between it and anything we would recognize as human intelligence. Part of the problem with AI is the way the rhetorical and cultural force of the term 'artificial intelligence' gets used to legitimate changes to social relations; seeing AI as nothing more than elaborate statistical guesswork goes some way towards making those changes more open to question.

Another reason we pay close attention to the particular dynamics of deep learning is because of the mutual articulation of technological and social forms. AI's technical operations are prefigurative of its wider effects, especially where the social and political conditions resonate with it: the patterns in the data and algorithms have their corollaries in the social relationships that surround them. So, while the focus of this chapter is on how AI actually works, we will see a tendency for it to propagate patterns of carelessness and extractiveness alongside a concentration and centralization of power. These insights lay the groundwork for Chapter 2 to expand on AI's wider political consequences.

Machine learning

The ideal to which AI strives is the dream of machine autonomy, but the technologies that exist right now under the banner of AI are, even at their most advanced, simply a version of what we call machine learning. Machine learning is distinguished from traditional programming by the fact that, instead of a programmer specifying the sequence of operations which produce the desired result, machine learning algorithms are fed a sample of the required results and use statistical estimation to figure out how to reproduce them.

The way the algorithm works out how to reproduce the results is not dissimilar to the way a straight line is fitted to a set of scattered points on a graph using a mathematical method. If a teacher gave you this task in school, you could probably do it pretty effectively by eye without doing any maths – you'd look at the dots, see roughly in which direction they were scattered, put a ruler on the paper at that angle, maybe shift it around a bit so there's a similar spread of points on both sides of the ruler, and draw your line. In general, a computer lacks all of the capacities you called on to do this; all it has access to is the coordinates of the points, so it has to use a mathematical method. It starts by drawing a random line, calculates the distance between each point and the line, shifts the line in a direction that makes the next guess better by reducing the total of all the distances, and repeats this over and over again until it's minimized the distance from the points to the fitted line.

More complex versions of the same kind of mathematical estimation are at the heart of machine learning. It isn't what most people would intuitively understand as 'learning': rather than the assimilation of novel concepts based on accumulated experience and common sense, machine learning is a set of mathematical operations of iteration and optimization. While machine learning has some clever mathematical tricks up its sleeve, it's important to grasp that it is a brute force mathematical process. There's no actual intelligence in artificial intelligence.

Machine learning improves a program's measurable performance on a narrow set of tasks by being given plenty of examples to learn from, usually in the form of large sets of labelled training data. It turns out that certain kinds of machine learning, when given enough training data and when running on powerful enough computers, can leverage numerical operations into an uncanny emulation of various human capacities, such as the ability to identify faces or to play strategy board games like Go. Of course, the computer is not 'recognizing' faces because it has no idea what the meaning of a face is, nor is it actually 'playing' anything, but even a decent imitation of these capacities by a dumb machine is impressive, and has certainly contributed to the sense of there having been a profound breakthrough in the quest for truly intelligent machines. However, as we will explore in more detail in later chapters, the very idea that there is such a thing as machine intelligence has deep social and political resonances. One of the most important aspects of machine learning is not that it heralds the sudden spark of consciousness in silicon but that it is a set of computational methods with political implications.

Data

Of all the entanglements between AI and society, perhaps the easiest to grasp is its dependency on data and the way that it might pick up unwanted patterns. There are many ways in which the training data can distort the outcomes of a machine learning algorithm. If the training data isn't a good representation of the data that the machine learning will actually encounter when in use then the algorithm will produce unanticipated outcomes. If a facial recognition algorithm is primarily trained on a dataset of White faces, for example, it will struggle when asked to recognize Black faces (Buolamwini and Gebru, 2018). One response to this might be that not being fairly represented in a dataset is analogous to not being fairly represented in a democratic system, which implies similar consequences in terms of second-class treatment. A logical demand would then be for more inclusive systems, in terms of their accuracy and the make-up of the dataset. The analogy isn't straightforward though, as inclusion isn't always an unalloyed good. The seemingly inevitable deployment of facial recognition by the police and other institutionally racist organizations, for example, has led some people to argue in favour of being left out of the data as much as possible (Samudzi, 2019).

There's no doubt that datasets that don't fully represent the real world are a problem for any deep learning system. As we'll see in Chapter 2, their inability to adapt to scenarios even slightly outside of the training data causes significant amounts of collateral damage. A deeper problem, though, is the very idea of representation that these systems propagate. This is well illustrated by the paradigmatic deep learning dataset called ImageNet, which consists of more than 14 million labelled images, each of which is tagged as belonging to one of more than 20,000 categories, or classes. The assumption that drove the creation of the dataset was of an unambiguous labelling; a set of terms that would describe an image correctly, and which would apply to any and all instances where that image crops up in the world. In this one sweeping gesture, ImageNet amputated the idea of a standpoint and asserted the irrelevance of context or embodied experience. A system trained on such a dataset knows nothing of history, power or meaning, so that a photo of 'an Israeli soldier holding down a young Palestinian boy while the boy's family try to remove the soldier' can be assigned the caption, 'People sitting on top of a bench together' (Katz, 2020).

This carelessness towards perspective and standpoint also applies to the labour of labelling these images. The only realistic way to create a database on this scale is to use crowdsourcing, and ImageNet images were labelled by the low paid, outsourced platform workers of Amazon's Mechanical Turk. Yet nothing of the contribution of these workers is acknowledged or granted any agency; rather they are characterized, where they are mentioned at all, as interchangeable sets of eyeballs. Anything that might identify them as having situated experience that would affect the way they label the images is ignored in favour of constructing an objectivist and universal formulation of vision at the cheapest possible cost (Denton et al, 2021). Yet the unmatched size of ImageNet made it pivotal for the evolution of computer vision. In 2012, the competition based on the dataset, the ImageNet Large Scale Visual Recognition Challenge, was won by a deep learning neural network that 'outperformed all other competitors by a previously unimaginable margin' (Babbage, 2010) and sparked the rise of deep learning across all domains.

The unrelenting demand for ever greater quantities of training data has sent existing mechanisms of data capture into overdrive.

Rather than accounting for the underlying assumptions about the elements of the world being datafied, the fixity of those elements over time and the robustness of their relationships, or the inevitable slippage between labels and their objects, the solution touted for fixing any problematic outcomes from the algorithms is to collect even more data. As well as driving an increase in data surveillance across the whole of society, one consequence is to turn the data searchlight more intensely onto the marginalized populations who, because of the way society is structured, already bear a disproportionate burden of intrusive data gathering. In their quest for scale, machine learning datasets consistently exhibit a callous instrumentalism towards their data subjects and a carelessness towards embedded values. Even when they're not missing some important range of real-world occurrences, the datasets of deep learning are dangerously reductive. They enforce a false equivalence between data point and label, which reverberates through the machine learning models built on top of them, because these latent simplifications overlap with correspondingly reductive social models.

The sudden leap in accuracy exhibited by deep learning when identifying ImageNet images is seen as the moment of take-off for contemporary AI and has helped to define machine learning orthodoxy. 'Thus, the 2012 ImageNet challenge did not simply showcase the high performance of deep learning, it also marked a shift in how researchers thought progress would be made. More and more people began to believe that the field could make significant progress simply by scaling up datasets' (Dotan and Milli, 2020). But this in itself creates barriers for entry, with implications for who gets to use AI and for what purposes. A dependency on large datasets further shifts the balance of AI power to entities with the capacity to collect and process massive quantities of data. Whatever we think of specific AI applications, accepting AI means we are implicitly signing up for an environment of pervasive data surveillance and centralized control.

Optimization

The purpose of all this data gathering is to furnish the raw material for optimization. The essential components of a machine learning system are a way to calculate the difference between its prediction and the training data (known as the loss function) and a way to iteratively improve on it (the optimizer). The role of the optimizer is to iterate repeatedly over the training data until it has minimized the loss function. When the loss function has been minimized, the machine learning system is considered to be trained; it now has a model for how to transform input data into classifications which can be interpreted as predictions.

In this way, humanly meaningful questions such as "does this patient have cancer" or "should we give this applicant the job?" are converted into activities that computers are good at: carrying out many thousands of repetitive calculations. In practice, a minimum may never be reached completely and the system will just carry on going while producing smaller improvements or even overfitting, so the researcher must decide when it's been training long enough and at what point to call a halt to its learning. A large part of the technical effort in machine learning is devoted to getting the most accurate results from the minimization of the loss function. What is less examined is what might be lost from sight by orienting our institutions around these kinds of algorithms.

Machine learning embeds the idea that the way to solve a problem is to find an objective to optimize on. Optimization is a particular kind of rationality, one that requires the context to be datafied and asserts that condensing its complexity into a calculation provides a superior kind of solution. Machine learning's optimizations are a kind of abstract utilitarianism, a mode of calculative ordering that results in particular ways of structuring systems. The logic of optimization, which has deep Cold War roots, already underpins our systems of logistics and planning, and the combination of granular data and machine learning opens up the opportunity for it to be used for social problems. The new era of machine learning means that a similar overarching logic to that which revolutionized global supply chains, through the abstraction and datafication made possible by containerization, can now be applied directly to everyday life.

Prior to the advent of deep learning, one thing that was holding machine learning back from widespread adoption was the difficulty of crafting accurate models for messy social contexts. While there are different kinds of machine learning algorithms, such as decision trees and support vector machines, they mostly need to be carefully tuned to get the best results. In particular, the analyst has to choose the right set of input features for the algorithm to use in its optimization, a process known as feature engineering. There are many problems where even careful feature engineering seems to lead to defeat, especially in areas like visual perception, facial recognition, and text or language comprehension. As much of an art as a science, effective feature engineering requires some element of domain expertise, that is, some grounded knowledge of the area to which the algorithm is being applied. Machine learning practitioners were forced to approach problems with some degree of deliberation, like it or not. That was radically changed by the arrival of deep learning, which in addition to delivering revolutionary accuracy also released the field of AI from having to grapple too closely with the awkward complexity of concrete situations.

Neural networks

Deep learning is a kind of machine learning based on multi-layer neural networks. Neural networks may be the cutting edge of contemporary AI, but they are not a new technology. US Air Force research psychologist and AI pioneer Frank Rosenblatt published the first papers on the Perceptron algorithm, an elementary form of neural network, in 1958, and it was actually turned into working hardware as an array of 20×20 light sensitive cells connected to the 'neurons' (actually, potentiometers) by a spaghetti-like sprawl of random wiring connections. This Mark I Perceptron could learn to recognize simple patterns, a definite breakthrough for its time. It was also characterized by two other features that have been pretty continuous over the history of AI: first, that this breakthrough was over-hyped and subsequent developments were disappointing, and second, that AI research was funded by the military for its own purposes.

The original aim of artificial neural networks was to emulate learning in the brain, which was understood to come from a progressive strengthening of patterns of connections between neurons. This model of how the brain learns was pithily paraphrased as "cells that fire together, wire together". An artificial neural network consists of at least one hidden layer of artificial neurons between the input data and the output layer. In a basic deep learning network, each element of input data is passed to all the neurons in the first hidden layer, multiplied by a positive or negative weight that reflects the strength of that particular connection. The signals at each neuron, which come from all the neurons in the prior level, are summed and modulated by a so-called activation function. The result becomes the output of that particular neuron, which in turn is passed on to every neuron in the next layer, again multiplied by a unique weight for each connection, where it is again summed and modulated before it is passed on to all the neurons in the next layer, and so on and so on to the output layer. The layers of neurons in these fully connected networks are usually represented in diagrams as serried ranks of small circles, where each row of neurons is wired to the next by the tightly woven lines of their interconnections. The signals travel along all of the myriad routes between the input neurons on one side and the output neurons on the other, modulated and distorted at each hidden layer as they are transformed from original data into prediction. The artificial neuron in the output layer with the largest total signal becomes the network's prediction. The strengths of each of the individual weights in all these myriad connections is what the neural network learns when it is trained, a process we'll look at a bit more closely in a moment. While it's highly unlikely that this arrangement represents the workings of any actual organic brain, it can still pull off some very clever mathematical pattern finding, and that's enough to make some believe it could be the basis for real machine intelligence.

The mathematical power of neural networks comes from their universality: in other words, for any input they can approximate the desired output function. As dry as 'being able to compute any function' may sound, it becomes a lot more compelling when you consider that translating a Chinese text into English can be thought of as computing a function, or taking a movie file and generating a description of the plot can be thought of as computing a function (Nielsen, 2019). Neural networks can, in principle, compute any function that maps from an input space to an output space. Of course, there's a world of difference between being able to do something in principle and being able to implement it in practice. For most of their history, neural networks and the wider field that they were part of, known as connectionist AI, were the poor relations of a different kind of AI system based on top-down rules and heuristics, known as symbolic AI. Where symbolic AI tried to model the way we think, connectionist AI tried to model the way our brains work. However, the computations required for connectionist AI meant that training a neural network could take weeks, so practical neural networks were largely neglected.

Around 2012 the conjunction of increased computing power, new algorithms and the glut of training data coming from the internet led to transformative advances in the multi-layer neural networks of deep learning. The advance in computing hardware was largely down to the Graphics Processing Unit (GPU), a class of chip that was originally developed to meet the gaming industry's demand for 3D graphics: it turned out that the same kind of matrix operations that render game environments could be adapted to train neural networks. One of the first deep learning models trained on a GPU was AlexNet, the deep learning system that produced the much heralded leap in accuracy on the ImageNet database (Krizhevsky et al, 2012).

The excitement generated by the new success of deep learning wasn't confined to the idea of efficient machine vision. With deep learning networks, you don't need to worry about which features of the training data to use, or whether you understand the nuances of the context, you just need to force enough training data through the layers and apply a method of optimization called stochastic gradient descent (of which more in a moment). Deep learning can find patterns in data that we can't even put into words – the kinds of patterns that have always been intractable to analytical description. Deep learning has been a breakthrough for facial recognition, speech recognition and language translation, and it's because of deep learning that we have smart home assistants and self-driving cars. It's fair to say that, in the perception of many practitioners, there are no apparent limits to the application of deep learning to complex problems. The deep learning pioneers, the ones who stuck with it in the wilderness years, believe that better neural network architectures will eventually lead to a re-creation of all aspects of human intelligence, including symbolic manipulation, causal inference and common sense (Dickson, 2021).

Transformations

It's worth pondering for a minute how neural networks are actually capturing and transforming the world; as we'll see in Chapter 2, these technical operations are closely coupled to social and political consequences. The first step in making the world available to a neural network is to encode the input data as a vector or a tensor. A vector is simply a column of numbers where each element represents an input feature. Tensors are expansions of vectors from two into three (or more) dimensions. Let's say we're dealing with a video: each pixel in a frame is represented by a value for red, green and blue, and the video is really a stack of these frames. So, when representing the video as numbers, the input to the algorithm is a huge, multidimensional block of data. As the input is passed through a deep learning network, the successive layers enact statistically driven distortions and transformations of the data, as the model tries to distill the latent information into output predictions. The intermediary layers enact various convolutions and reductions of the input block, stretching and compressing it until the output can be flattened into a set of predictions.

Everything that passes through a neural network in this way is represented as a number: if the original data is categorical, meaning it comes in descriptive classes labelled by words, it is still converted into vectors of numbers. However diverse the input data, the cross-connections in the layers munge it together into one interwoven distribution. The long history of statistical reasoning shows how state and non-state institutions have always used statistical methods to turn the diversity of lived experience into a single space of equivalence, ready for distant decision-making (Desrosières, 2010). The statistical transformations of AI are the latest iteration in this process of rendering the world ready for algorithmic governance.

In our already metricized world, we're familiar with complex aspects of our experience being made commensurable: that is, turned into numbers for comparison and ranking, whether that's in a national league table of school performance or in the number of stars we give for an online product review. AI makes aspects of the world commensurable, then vectorizes, transforms and recombines them. It's immaterial to a neural network whether the data passing through it represents the corpus of Shakespeare's plays or a week's worth of traffic flow in London – it's a set of numbers that must be mathematically traded against each other as the network tries to minimize its loss function. What this also opens up, as we will explore in more detail in Chapter 2, is opportunities for unaccountable decisions, unjust exclusions and exploitative speculations.

Backpropagation

When discussing some of the issues that arise from deep learning networks, like transparency, explainability and control, it will be useful to have a sense of the scale of their operations. The signal from each neuron in one layer is multiplied by a particular weight at a given neuron in the next layer, so if one layer in a neural network has 64 neurons, and each is being fed an input signal from all of the 128 neurons in the layer above, the number of weights in that layer alone is $64 \times 128 = 8,192$. It's these weights that get modified in order to better minimize the output of the loss function. Modern neural networks have complex architectures including, for example, convolutional layers, which are basically sliding filters that amplify particular patterns. The AlexNet network architecture from 2012 consisted of a stack of convolutional layers and fully connected layers with a total number of 62,378,344 adjustable weights, and the numbers of parameters in cutting edge AI models have gone up sharply since then.

The simple number of weights doesn't even represent the full scale of operations, because we use iterative methods to optimize them. Each time it processes a batch of training data, the optimizer guesses the values of the weights and changes them slightly to improve the next guess, so it ends up looping across each weight hundreds or even thousands of times. A key part of this process is the backpropagation algorithm, which calculates gradients of change that represent the direction of improvement. The difference between the predicted outputs and the target values is used to calculate layer-by-layer gradients of change, starting with the changes needed in the final layer, using that to calculate changes needed in the next-to-last layer, and so on and so on, sweeping back across the network. Once all the gradients have been calculated the optimizer works out how best to alter the entire galaxy of weights in the right direction for the next iteration.

If your eyes glaze over somewhat when trying to visualize all these processes, don't worry; deep learning is a complex set of nested mathematical operations that are off the scale in terms of anything we can grasp directly. All we're trying to do here is get a bit of a handle on the inner reasoning of neural networks so that we can assess the legitimacy of applying them to different kinds of problems. The way a neural network uses backpropagation and the loss function to 'reason' its way to an optimal solution is known as stochastic gradient descent: if, overall, the loss is represented as points on a landscape, then gradient descent can be visualized as the network inching its way down the slope of the abstract loss landscape in small random steps, as it seeks the bottom of a valley that represents the minimum loss. This may be a mathematically tractable method, but the landscape rarely consists of a unique valley, and can be filled with various dips and crevices that will trap an unwary algorithm. At the very least, this invisible complexity should cast doubt on any claim made by deep learning to produce a singular truth.

In deep learning's forward–backward sweep of prediction–correction, it seems like the process of weaving back and forth has followed the history of programmable systems, from the first Jacquard weaving looms of the early nineteenth century, which were controlled by punched cards, to the deep learning systems of the twenty-first century. Given the number of weights to be minimized and the repetitive passing back and forth, it's obvious that backpropagation is complex and must be computationally demanding, but it is not a black box process; we can examine the values of the weights at any stage. The real challenge is interpreting these millions of weights in a way that is accessible to human reasoning. The network can't tell us why a particular pattern in any layer is significant: it delivers a prediction, not an explanation. So, while neural networks can extract predictions from messy input data with uncanny effectiveness, they paradoxically cast a long shadow over our chances of understanding any trade-offs they make in the process. As we'll see in the next chapter, this has deep implications for the distribution of real-world benefits and harms.

Infrastructure

Neural network models are forged by the millions of calculations that occur during their optimization. While the diagrams of AI architectures may, to outsiders, look like abstract hieroglyphics, the computations are a wholly material process. Each semiconductor logic gate on a silicon chip needs a tiny electrical kick to change state, and there are millions of these events happening every second inside the racks of warehoused servers that provide the necessary computing resource. As anyone who owns a gaming PC will know, GPU chips draw even more power than regular Central Processing Units (CPUs), and cloud computing sets this up on an industrial scale: if artificial intelligence has a soundtrack, it's the deafening whir of cooling fans in the server farms. The amount of processing power needed to train AI models (the number of actual calculations involved) is going up exponentially: between AlexNet, the image classification algorithm from 2012, and AlphaGo, the AI that beat a top-ranking player at Go in 2016, the number of computing operations required for model training went up by a factor of 300,000 (Open AI, 2018a). AI is not only a matter of computation but a significant commitment of material resources.

The energy demands of AI don't only come from the scale of the operations of optimization but from the fact that the whole training loop is repeated many times in order to find the best model. There are always choices to be made about the number and size of layers, their types and arrangements, and other settings, like 'learning rate', which are to do with the optimization algorithm. These variables are collectively known as hyperparameters, and finding the most accurate model means optimizing networks with different hyperparameters to see which one performs the best.

One of the latest language models at the time of writing, called GPT-3, has 175 billion weights that need to be optimized. Training its cousin, the BERT algorithm, which is used for natural language inference, has the same carbon emissions as a trans-American flight, while using a method called 'neural architecture search' to optimize the hyperparameters of a similar model produces the same carbon emissions as five cars over their entire lifetimes (Strubell et al, 2019). Some of these refinements are for the sake of the very marginal improvements in overall accuracy, more related to cut-throat competition between industry research labs than practical utility. Curiously enough, given the gung ho manner with which the AI industry sucks up all available data to train its models, one kind of data that it refuses to make available in return is key data about its overall energy consumption (Belkhir and Elmeligi, 2018). Nevertheless, the carbon emissions are clearly significant enough that AI should be factored into future decisions about tackling climate change.

The ability to understand the world through AI, and to intervene in it, is increasingly the domain of those with the capacity to develop the biggest models, and even academics who are leading the research need access to the large-scale computing power of private industry. AI research is largely privatized, or at least wholly dependent on the cloud computing resources of Amazon Web Services (AWS), Google Cloud, Microsoft Azure or Alibaba Cloud. Even the CIA now depends on the cloud infrastructure of AWS (Konkel, 2016). It may in fact be that one of the attributes of AI that governing institutions find so appealing, alongside novel applications and the dream of machine intelligence, is its innate centralization and the barriers to entry it creates. The resources required to develop cutting-edge deep learning models are not only matters of environmental justice but of social power.

Crowdsourcing

Steep gradients of social power also mark the background labour that makes deep learning possible. Contemporary deep learning systems are mostly forms of supervised learning, which means they need training data, which in turn means someone has to do the labour of labelling that data. While there is a shift towards unsupervised models, especially in natural language processing, there is still a fundamentally extractive relationship between the original human activity of data creation and its use in deep learning. Some of this need is satisfied by the free labour we unknowingly provide online, for example by tagging our friends in photos on social media, but the bulk of the work is carried out by a poorly paid and largely invisible workforce. This has been the case since the beginning of computation; as Simon Schaffer writes about the nineteenth-century calculating machines: 'To make machines look intelligent it was necessary that the sources of their power, the labour force which surrounded and ran them, be rendered invisible' (Schaffer, 1994).

AI as we now know it depends on crowdsourced click-workers mobilized through platforms like Crowdflower or Amazon's Mechanical Turk. These intermediaries supply and manage cheap labour so that the AI companies who are busy developing advanced tech need have nothing to do with them. Thanks to the affordances of the internet, many of these workers are based in the Global South, and it's these forms of globally distributed labour that make it economically viable to produce the required volumes of labelled data, whether that's tagging images from social media or transcribing voice recordings from systems like Siri and Alexa. As a result, low-waged women workers in Kenyan click-farms spend all day drawing bounding boxes to identify objects in road scenes, helping to train self-driving cars that they will never get to ride in (Lee, 2018). Such is the scale of the market for self-driving car data that specialist crowdsourcing firms have emerged who guarantee the accuracy required, and take advantage of situations like the economic collapse in Venezuela to tap into pools of well-educated people who have suddenly dropped into poverty and are desperate for even this precarious work (Chen, 2019). Signing up to AI as we know it means deepening a commitment to labour practices that most of us aren't even aware of, that are gendered and racialized, and that come without any collective negotiation of fair conditions or remuneration.

Perhaps the dependency of AI on extractive labour practices should come as no surprise, given the much vaunted ancestry of computing in the Difference Engine and the Analytical Engine, those mechanical creations of Charles Babbage. Babbage was not only a theorist of early computing but of the early factory system – the unifying factor in both cases being the division of labour. He hailed the advance of 'manufacture' over mere making based on the division and analytical regulation of the work process in the factory (Babbage, 2010). The aim of his 1832 book, *On the Economy of Machinery and Manufactures*, was to demonstrate 'the most economical recompense to each component in terms of consumed power (if mechanical) or consumed wages (if human)' (Schaffer, 1994). In the preface to the book on factories he says, 'The present volume may be considered as one of the consequences that have resulted from the Calculating-Engine, the construction of which I have been so long superintending' (Babbage, 2010, p iii). Dividing complex calculations into small steps enabled them to be mechanized, while dividing workers' labour into simplified steps enabled extractive efficiency and worker surveillance.

Another notable continuity between that time and the present day is the long arc of anti-worker sentiment that stretches from Charles Babbage to, for example, Jeff Bezos and today's Amazon corporation. In the abovementioned volume, Babbage wrote that 'one great advantage which we derive from machinery is the check which it affords against the inattention, idleness or the dishonesty of human agents', and he argued that trade union combination was always 'injurious' to the workforce. Amazon actively monitors the 'risk' that its operations will become unionized (Leon, 2020), and fired staff protesting against unsafe working conditions during the pandemic (Evelyn, 2020). A former vice president of Amazon revealed to *The New York Times* that founder Jeff Bezos believes workers are 'inherently lazy' (Kantor et al, 2021) and that this overriding belief shaped the systems of AI-driven worker control that pervade Amazon warehouses and delivery operations.

This chapter began with the minimization of the loss function but ended on the shopfloor of the Amazon warehouse. AI's operations are never abstract but always entangled in social relations of power. In this chapter we've explored some of the detail of AI's technical workings in order to unearth its connections to specific forms of social patterning, and to material and political consequences. We've seen how clever its methods can be but also what can become lost and uncared for in the process. In the following chapters we will expand this focus on social and political implications, looking in turn at the immediate fall-out of AI's brittle solutions, at what happens when it is taken up at scale by institutions, and at the role it is likely to play under conditions of increasing social and global crisis.

2

Collateral Damage

This chapter makes the case that, far from being a useful technical innovation that simply needs to be cleared of bias, AI is a brittle and opaque form of statistical reasoning that reinforces social inequality. The chapter breaks this down into three main themes: the fragility of AI, the way this manifests in practice as injustice, and the consequent problems with applying AI as a solution to social problems.

One of the reasons people get excited about AI is because of the way it can be applied to so many different challenges. However, the characteristics of abstraction and optimization that make AI so appealing also make it brittle in ways that amount to statistical callousness. Its operations easily become forms of social profiling and targeting that act as 'solutionism', that is, as technical fixes that cover up underlying structural unfairness.

The AI industry would have us believe that any ensuing injustice is simply a side effect that can be regulated out, but claims that AI can be constrained by a human in the loop or by legal frameworks are overridden by the way it acts in concert with institutional power. The harms caused by AI solutions are forms of collateral damage that fall most heavily on the already marginalized.

Brittleness

AI is presented by its advocates as deriving profound insights from the world, but there are plenty of signs that these insights can be distorted and unreliable. The statistical nature of machine learning means it assumes that the distribution of data on which the algorithm has been trained covers the spread of occurrences in the wider world. Any shift in the underlying distribution (new behaviours, unexpected events) can throw a spanner in the works. There have been cases where a self-driving car has collided with a tow truck at the side of the road because its training data didn't include a statistically significant representation of tow trucks (Charrington, 2019).

Even when neural networks seem to understand the world around them, it turns out to be a shallow understanding. The way a deep learning network learns to recognize objects, for example, is by being shown many example images of said objects. It doesn't develop an embodied understanding of their physicality by living among them, as we do, so even a simple rotation of objects can throw its recognition abilities into disarray, as with the high-end object classification system that confidently decides an overturned school bus is not a school bus at all but a snow plough (Alcorn et al, 2019). It turns out that all but the most mundane of images need a background understanding that is missing from AI, which is why, 'to these systems, an image of people escaping a flood may look like "people on a beach," and a crashing airplane like "an airplane on a tarmac"' (Katz, 2020).

Founding figures of deep learning acknowledge that, while AI can perform well on specific tasks, the systems 'are often brittle outside of the narrow domain they have been trained on' (Bengio et al, 2021). And yet, as philosophers since the Greeks have been at pains to point out, one thing we can be really sure of is that the world is constantly changing. Any AI in the real world is going to be faced with unexpected examples, whether it's navigating the chaos of traffic or deciding on unique immigration applications. AI, it seems, is both powerful and fragile. It is striking that the first pedestrian killed by a self-driving car, a high-end Volvo being used by Uber as a test vehicle, was crossing the road while laboriously pushing a bicycle laden with their shopping bags. The question we should be asking of all real-world applications of AI is who will pay the price for their fragilities?

Problems arise not only from the training distribution but from the dependency on proxy measures. Very often, we can't directly measure the things that matter the most, like happiness or health, so algorithms have to rely on proxies. As an example, consider the algorithm used by several large hospitals in the USA to predict which patients are likely to benefit from high-risk care management, which takes the data from previous health insurance claims as a proxy for health risk. A study with access to insurance claims and actual hospital data for thousands of patients discovered that, while the algorithm's risk score showed no bias in its distribution in relation to White people or Black people at a given risk level, the actual health burden of Black people was significantly greater (Obermeyer et al, 2019). At a given level of predicted risk, Black patients were two to three times sicker. The underlying fact, which was opaque to the algorithm, was that Black people get much sicker before they're likely to make an insurance claim, and not taking this into account meant that choosing a seemingly unbiased proxy for health ended up discriminating against Black patients by not offering them help until they were much more ill. The algorithm unintentionally propagated hidden inequities in existing healthcare. The authors conclude that 'the choice of convenient, seemingly effective proxies for ground truth can be an important source of algorithmic bias in many contexts' (Obermeyer et al, 2019, p 447).

Far too often, the 'ground truth' that machine learning practitioners cite as validation for their models is determined without going anywhere near the ground and without asking anyone at ground level what their truth might be. As a result, seemingly rational proxies can splinter on the sharp cliffs of existing structural inequality. The 'convenience' in the case of this health algorithm comes, in part, from not having to engage with structural legacies of colonialism and slavery, and 'seemingly effective' refers to the logic of a completely marketized health system. As we'll see in Chapter 3, when we look at the relationship of AI to welfare, algorithms can amplify the tendency of bureaucracies to rely on sweeping generalizations for policy enforcement while ignoring the messy inconveniences of lived experience.

Proxies are not the only pitfall for deep learning, as neural networks also have an innate tendency to cheat. Recall that the operation of a deep learning algorithm is to optimize, and that it is architectured to make this as efficient as possible: in the absence of any constraint, the network will learn literally any pattern that enables it to optimize on the training data. 'It's in the nature of optimisation problems that as it's free to play with variables outside the utility function, it will often set them to extreme values' (CRASSH Cambridge, 2015). In the case of object recognition, this may be achieved by correctly identifying the object or by picking up on a shortcut, like a difference in the backgrounds or in the image textures, as in the apocryphal story of the neural network that correctly spots camouflaged tanks in the forest because all of the photos with tanks in were taken on cloudy days and the non-tank scenes were mostly sunny (Branwen, 2011). No shortcut is too trivial for the algorithm to exploit if it can.

Non-visual applications of AI have analogous ways of cheating, and the problem is usually only revealed when the system is applied outside the test dataset, where the 'cheat' features are not present. Surprisingly, perhaps, this isn't something that can ever be completely eliminated: 'Models always base their decisions on reduced information and thus generalization failures should be expected' (Jacobsen et al, 2020). This way of forcing a solution by whatever means is not innocent when it comes to social applications. Deep neural networks 'will often find solutions no matter whether the task is well-substantiated. For instance, they might try to find a shortcut to assess credit-scores from sensitive demographics (e.g. skin color or ethnicity) or gender from superficial appearance' (Jacobsen et al, 2020). As we'll see when we look at physiognomy and race science, deep learning can unfortunately cook up an answer to deplorable questions that are not based on science or causality but which are only being asked in order to deepen problematic power relations.

The fact that neural networks have uncanny ways of failing as well as uncanny powers is neatly captured by the existence of adversarial examples. A typical adversarial example in object recognition is a pair of images: one will be a clearly identifiable object, such as a tortoise, and the other will be the same image with a faintly perceptible speckling or noise. The AI will correctly identify the first as a tortoise and will confidently categorize the second as something utterly different, for example an AR-15 rifle

(Athalye et al, 2018). Of course, the 'noise' that produces this effect is not random; it uses insider knowledge of the algorithm to craft a signal that messes with it by subtly altering the image so that the learned gradients of the machine learning model push it into a different category. However, no toddler presented with the altered image would make the same mistake.

This is not a superficial fragility nor is it one that's easily fixed – it goes to the heart of the system's 'learning' about the world. The neural network has learned how to efficiently map labelled examples of human perception, and it seems to us that the network learns to recognize things the way that we do. But the training dataset, no matter how large, is a small cluster of the unimaginably large data space of possible input images. The system will take any of those possible inputs, even if they look to us like garbled nonsense, and confidently assign them to a 'most likely' category. A clever mathematical search for adversarial examples can therefore find images that are somewhat similar to our inputs but which our model will tip into an incorrect classification (Geng and Veerapaneni, 2019). The neural network isn't really failing when it labels the tortoise as an AR-15, it's just that it has efficiently learned how to do something in a brittle and non-adaptive way (OpenAI, 2017). Adversarial examples make it clear that whatever patterns AI is learning in order to classify images, they strongly diverge from human perception. The question that haunts AI is what adversarial outcomes will emerge when its applied to intervene in social patterns.

Fixes

Picking up on deep learning's eccentricities is made harder by its opacity. There's a trade-off between accuracy and explainability, whereby neural networks often make more accurate predictions than other kinds of machine learning but, because of the complex abstractions in the hidden layers, it's hard to know why. That makes it tricky to know what they might then go on to do in real-world situations. For example, one neural network accurately predicted which pneumonia patients would develop complications, however the same network insisted patients with underlying asthma should be sent straight home without treatment (Caruana et al, 2015). The AI had learned the pattern from the data because, in actual fact, asthma sufferers with pneumonia usually get sent straight to intensive care, and thanks to this, hardly ever develop serious complications. The AI had learned a true pattern, but what it had learned, in effect, was that asthma lowers risk.

The neural network in itself was too opaque for the researchers to be able to reverse engineer its reasoning, and its test results looked fine because it was correctly predicting most complications. The industry knows that explainability is a potential Achilles' heel for AI and is pouring resources into it, but due to the intractable density of deep learning, the explanatory methods are essentially a form of post-hoc guesswork. In the case of the pneumonia algorithm, it was only because the researchers were also using a simpler and more interpretable model alongside the neural network that they were able to spot what was going on. 'If there hadn't been an interpretable model', one of the researchers cautioned, 'you could accidentally kill people' (Bornstein, 2016).

Explainability efforts are an instance of the technical fix: trying to correct problems with advanced algorithms by applying more algorithms. Word embeddings are a good example both of the way deep learning embeds deep discrimination and of attempts to correct that on a technical level. Word embeddings underpin the way a search engine interprets our queries, and also the way that online translation works. An embedding takes all the words from a giant corpus of text and boils them down to vectors in a relatively small dimensional space. In AI, a vector simply means an entity with more than one element: so, in this case, each word gets represented by a column of numbers. Any vector can be thought of as something with size and direction, like an arrow, and the word vectors are related in a way that maps onto language use. For example, in vector terms, 'king' − 'man' + 'woman' = 'queen'. This gives mathematical methods like AI, which have no understanding of language as such, access to a manipulable proxy for meaning. Unfortunately the vectors also inherit the social assumptions embedded in statistical patterns of word use, so that, as the title of a well-known paper that analyzes these embeddings puts it when referring to the vector relationships that the authors discovered in their study, 'Man is to Computer Programmer as Woman is to Homemaker' (Bolukbasi et al, 2016).

As concerning as this embedded cultural prejudice might seem, the drive for AI to succeed means that findings like these are seen less as a problem and more as an opportunity. Having identified bias mathematically, the thinking goes, it can be mathematically corrected by shifting values to remove it. All problematically gendered terms can be zeroed along the gender axis in data space so they don't lean in a male or female direction. Lo and behold, algorithms go one better than humans because their prejudices can be instantly corrected. However, the drawback to this seductive proposition is that it's unclear what other distortions this so-called correction may amplify or introduce. This practice of mathematical 'debiasing' forges forward in blissful ignorance of the nuances of intersectionality, that is, of the contextual interplay of oppressions like gender, race, disability and so on. And because of the hubris of the AI field, it does so without seeking out the voices of those who are directly affected.

It's also possible to try to constrain potential injustice on a statistical level by monitoring the balance of outcomes. Take, for example, the COMPAS algorithm, which is a commercial software used in the US court system to generate a risk score for suspects being offered bail. Northpointe, the company that created the software, considers that their algorithm is fair because it has the same predictive accuracy across race; in any predicted risk category, the same percentage of White defendants and of Black defendants actually go on to reoffend. However a journalistic investigation of COMPAS showed that, although the algorithm's input data doesn't include ethnicity, Black defendants were twice as likely to be refused bail as White defendants with similar criminal records (Angwin et al, 2016; Larson et al, 2016). The likelihood of being unfairly detained versus the likelihood of reoffending are different quantifications of fairness. It turns out that it's mathematically impossible for the COMPAS algorithm to satisfy both ideas of fairness at the same time, given the background data of police contacts and arrests. No statistical balancing can address the question of justice because the root of the problem is the imbalance in the interactions of the police with the different communities.

Technical fixes make sense to computer and data scientists because they feel legitimated by aligning with the values of engineering and the ideals of scientific objectivity. Being disciplined into a science-like view of the world makes them believe that turning justice into maths is the way to avoid slipping into dangerous subjectivity. So concepts like fairness and equal opportunities are translated into formal metrics like 'disparate impact' (Selbst et al, 2018), where fairness can be measured as a mathematical distribution of benefits or harms. But, in the end, the root problem is seeing the computation as the structure that needs fixing rather than the structure of society itself.

An abstract framing of a messy social issue always fails to account for some of the underlying factors, while weighting others in ways that are hard for us to fully divine. Technical ingenuity becomes part of the problem rather than part of the solution. Rather than reflecting on the need to tackle the yawning chasm of structural power and discrimination that the machines are being trained on, the engineering approach is to 'fix' it with even more abstraction. But the operations of oppressive power can't be mathematically waved away. The mathematical characterization of difference can be weaponized as easily as it can be 'corrected', and it doesn't require a fascistic regime for this to happen. As we'll see in Chapter 3, when it comes to issues of race and racialization, the reduction of social and cultural complexity to a measurable distance in some abstract data space is a mechanism that inevitably amplifies injustice rather than correcting for it.

The notion of technical reforms might be an ineffective way to tackle structural injustice but it underpins a wider public relations narrative about ethical AI. The industry has reacted to emerging unease about AI in society by reaching for the cover of ethics, and there's been a nearly universal adoption of ethical principles by major AI companies to accompany the development of technical tools to fix the problem. Bias is presented as an invasive outsider that can be hunted down and cleansed while companies purify themselves by paying lip service to ethical philosophy.

AI corporations are prepared to pay a hefty fee to be seen as on the ethical side of history, and they've been funding ethics research centres left, right and centre. Even some of the non-profits who are busy critiquing AI have funding and staffing links to the same corporations. Google took advantage of its own staff's efforts to make AI ethical by offering ethics as a service (Simonite, 2020), although this was undermined by the way they subsequently sacked Timnit Gebru, their leading AI ethicist and a Black woman, for having the temerity to challenge their internal lack of progress on inclusion (Ingram, 2020). Google's self-evident hypocrisy, and its subsequent gaslighting and undermining of former staff, highlights the gulf between ethical statements and actual practice. The performative *mea culpa* of the corporate ethical turn isn't really intended to grasp the problems of AI at the root but to fend off both unwelcome legal regulation from above and any emergence of popular resistance from below.

From the corporations' point of view, lobbying for 'responsible AI' through alliances like the Partnership on AI (The Partnership on AI, 2016) is good business, whereas aligning with actual social movements that are tackling the inequality of social structures would be unthinkable. An ethical commitment is non-threatening and enables product release deadlines to proceed unimpeded. Ethics, as mobilized by corporates and their fellow travellers, is not only a matter of fine sounding statements but a method of depoliticizing and individualizing problems that should really be a matter of collective political concern. As with scientific fields like population genetics, where ethical principles 'play key roles in eliding fundamental social and political issues' (Reardon, 2011, cited in Green, 2020), it is seen as better for AI to focus on developing more inclusive datasets and adopting ethical frameworks than to face up to its role in structural injustice.

Injustice

As is becoming clear by now, socially applied AI has a tendency to punch down: that is, the collateral damage that comes from its statistical fragility ends up hurting the less privileged. This is reinforced by the fact that, in all likelihood, the people in the room when the algorithm gets designed will represent a privileged standpoint in society. Probabilistic algorithms have an inevitable flexibility in exactly where the decision boundaries are drawn, and can be tuned in many different ways on the journey through model development and deployment. This affects, for example, the balance of false positives (where an algorithm makes a wrong identification) and false negatives (where an algorithm misses something). Not only will design decisions be influenced by the outlook of the engineers but by the fact that the algorithms are being tuned at the behest of the powerful institutions that employ them.

What's being flexed in this way is not simply a pattern of numbers at an output layer but the resulting distribution of life experiences. It's one thing if that shift is limited to the contents of a social media feed, but the consequences become a lot more significant if the algorithm is shortlisting job candidates or selecting suspicious travellers at a border crossing. As a result of this overloading of social hierarchy in the design process, it should be no surprise that, as with police 'stop and search' operations, the generation of algorithmic false positives will both reflect existing social discrimination and act to reinforce it.

The question of discrimination is central to AI. It must be able to clearly discriminate in a technical sense, that is, to tell the difference between things at the level of data. Indeed, the purpose of the final layers in a neural network is to force the model to discriminate in favour of one of the labelled outcomes. It is equally clear from our look at deep learning so far that it has a tendency to discriminate in a social sense. Any closeness in data space can be interpreted as an innate affinity, and a machine learning prediction about someone won't be based on their individual comportment or intentions but the net behaviours of those they share attributes with. We are not the individual subjects of AI but the inferential subjects of AI. The shared structural characteristics picked up by AI are predictive, and therefore 'efficient', in the same way that gender is predictive of lower pay, or race is predictive of likelihood to be stopped by police while walking down the road. It's pattern recognition as self-reinforcing social profiling.

Tackling AI discrimination is made even more difficult by its aforementioned opacity. Deep learning sets up a collision between computational processes and due process, where due process is the longstanding principle of natural justice through which any judgement with significant impact offers the accused both a fair hearing and a full explanation. As we've seen, the strength of neural networks is that you just give them the data and they figure out the rules, but the catch is that they can't tell you what the rules are. If we can't understand exactly what is being weighed in the balance, it is very hard to tell under what circumstances individual harm may be caused or an injustice may be taking place.

When it perceives significant unease about the potential for algorithmic injustice, the AI industry falls back on the idea of the 'human in the loop': no need to worry about what those pesky algorithms might do, there'll be somebody keeping an eye on them. How much faith can we have in the proposition that a well-placed human will limit the scope of algorithmic harm? A human in the loop defuses the threatening idea of machines making decisions about people, but we might wonder whether this is enough to restrain the opaque but authoritative pronouncements of machine learning. There are many reasons why people might defer to an AI, even when they have doubts, but the key one will probably be where the algorithm is understood to be the manifestation of organizational priorities: in effect, the human in the loop will be overridden by the institution in the loop.

In fact, the human has far more to worry about from being in the loop than the AI does. When things go wrong it's likely to be the human that gets the blame, whether that's in scandal-prone professions like social work or simply the luckless human in a self-driving car accident. Many public services are high-stakes and high-pressure environments scorched by years of austerity, where the worker-in-the-loop is caught in a web composed of algorithms, regulations and institutional management. The human is the moral crumple zone, 'just as the crumple zone in a car is designed to absorb the force of impact in a crash, the human in a highly complex and automated system may become simply a component – accidentally or intentionally – that bears the brunt of the moral and legal responsibilities when the overall system malfunctions' (Elish, 2019, p 40). Moreover, shunting blame onto humans may well result in the conclusion that humans should be taken out of the pathway altogether, thus returning to the idea of machine-only decisions. Thus, AI can transcend human fallibility by setting the human up to fail. In the end, the real allure of AI for institutions is not that it is actually more accurate or objective than people but simply that it is never going to experience a moment of ethical doubt about what it's being asked to do. With humans in the loop, the smooth functioning of institutional processes that are discriminatory, unethical or unjust are always vulnerable to interruption from acts of individual conscience or collective refusal. With AI alone, no such risk exists.

If neither human discretion nor ethical principles can restrain algorithmic harmfulness, surely, some might say, we can at least rely on the law to protect us. What's needed is robust regulation, and where better to look for that than to the European Union (EU) and it's enlightened 'European values'. Unfortunately, the rhetoric of law-making efforts and their practical effects differ sharply, not least because of the political and industrial lobbying that takes place during their development. Laws like the EU's General Data Protection Regulation (GDPR) narrow and individualize the issues, whereas, particularly in the case of AI, the questions are profoundly communal. What are really needed to counter the ability of systems like deep learning to make invasive predictions are collective interventions, a point we'll return to in the later chapters of this book.

The current EU efforts to develop AI regulation are illustrative of the institutional self-interest that undermines real protection. The High Level Expert Group that advised on the law was dominated by industry representation, and the proposed AI Act favours corporate self-regulation, includes massive loopholes, and relies on technical checks on bias of the kind we discussed in the previous section (Chander and Jakubowska, 2021). Moreover, it does little to restrain the AI-powered surveillance systems that EU states deploy as part of their hostile border regimes – the same border regimes that are responsible for violent pushbacks in the Balkans and drownings in the Mediterranean. In producing the proposed law, the EU dumped its own 'red lines' of supposedly non-negotiable ethical principles (Metzinger, 2019), while the Act's detail diverts the rhetoric of protections into ineffective standards and irrelevant sub-clauses (Veale and Borgesius, 2021).

The fundamental problem with all attempts at legal regulation is not the debatable practicality of algorithmic accountability but the way a legal veneer already covers up for the discriminatory realities on the ground. Whatever jurisdiction we live in, we are surrounded by perfectly legal injustices that deepen every day. The law, like AI, is another technology that is not neutral. Laws against discrimination, for example, fail to address the intergenerational disadvantages of marginalization, highlighting the gulf between the limits of regulation and the absence of reparation. The 'rights' that the law instantiates are procedural, like the right to a due process, rather than substantive, such as the right to adequate housing or having enough to eat. So it's perfectly within the law that millions of children in a rich nation such as the UK live in poverty, that head teachers report, 'my children have grey skin, poor teeth, poor hair' (Richardson, 2018) and come into school hungry, and teachers have to supplement children's meagre lunches of bread and margarine while at the same time being pressured by the system to focus on algorithmically driven league tables. The law cannot correct for algorithmic injustice resulting from structural inequality because the law itself sustains those structures. Trying to repair these injustices through legal regulation simply provides the carceral system with more avenues of potential criminalization. It's not that law is failing to regulate the harmful effects of algorithms, but rather that algorithms are exposing the comprehensive failure of the law to address real injustice.

Socially applied AI systems are innate purveyors of injustice not only because they operate in an unjust system but also because they are indifferent to causality. Correlations measure how variables vary together: if a change in one variable is matched by a similar change in another then they are said to be highly correlated. The patterns that AI learns through its modelling are correlations, not causation: they pick out systematic coincidences rather than driving forces. The difference between correlation and causation is repeated endlessly to every undergraduate learning about statistics, in subjects from physics to psychology, so as to avoid mistaken explanations for the way things work. It's not that finding correlations is wrong as such, only mistaking them for causes: spotting meaningful correlations is an important part of the scientific process. The correlations found in AI may have meaning by, for example, reflecting real structural inequalities, and the way to draw this out would be to involve marginalized communities in the interpretation of the results. But reflective understanding is not the purpose of AI – its aim is simply to extract an effective basis for intervention.

The goal of AI is to predict and target, not to provide any sociological accounting for the reasons why people might seem to occupy particular patterns of life (Birhane and Cummins, 2019). AI isn't aiming for understanding: it only cares about what will come next, not why. Let loose on real data, AI will seek out correlations with implacable mathematical determination, and if it needs to enact new forms of discrimination or exclusion to achieve its goal it will do so. Its mathematical operations of ordering and ranking carry over into our daily lives as the distribution of benefits and sanctions, while the choice of what the AI should optimize on is made by those with accrued privilege and applied to those without it. In the end, the overarching correlation will be between the impacts of AI and the maintenance of existing social power, accompanied by the intensification of discriminative ordering.

Solutionism

Despite AI's potentially harmful fragilities and its tendency to couple closely to injustice, it is already seen as a way of solving social problems, and will particularly appeal to bureaucratic institutions charged with delivering society's services at scale. The algorithms will add an abstract thoughtlessness to existing institutional categorizations, which are already quite capable of channelling callousness. Consider, for example, the category of 'Troubled Family', which was introduced in 2012 by the UK government to tackle what they claimed were intergenerational patterns of anti-social behaviour. As the head of the Troubled Families programme said at the time, 'We are not running some cuddly social workers programme ... we should be talking about things like shame and guilt ... we have lost the ability to be judgmental because we worry about being seen as nasty to poor people' (Winnett and Kirkup, 2012). The government minister in charge said, 'We have sometimes run away from categorising, stigmatising, laying blame. We need a less understanding approach' (Lewell-Buck, 2017). There's a long historical precedent for ignoring structural problems by creating judgemental categories that blame the individual and attempt to discriminate between, for example, the 'deserving poor' and the 'undeserving poor'. If applied to automate similar efforts, AI will become a mode of algorithmic morality judgement.

AI will modulate social categorization in ways that are both familiar and unfamiliar. Classifications are part of the interlocking systems of meaning and control that shape our relationships with institutions and each other, and even shape the ways we think about ourselves and relate to our own embodied being (Spade, 2015), starting with the sweeping classifications of race, gender, sexuality, disability, social class and so on. When thinking about the broader impacts of AI and its associated datasets, it's not sufficient to question the way it might be misrepresenting of our authentic selves, but to realize that it will act to reconstruct us as a particular subject that it will then act upon.

An example of this is the Netradyne AI-driven camera array installed to monitor Amazon delivery drivers. Under the auspices of improved safety, much boasted about by Amazon spokespeople, this machine learning system is trained to generate various alerts related to distracted or unsafe driving. One such alert is triggered when the AI decides the van has drawn too close to the vehicle in front. The van drivers, however, say it is also triggered by a car pulling in front and cutting them off, even though they were driving safely (Gurley, 2021). These alerts cost drivers their rating and bonus because the automated surveillance is tied into the contractors' payment system; in effect, if the Netradyne AI says you are a bad driver, you *are* a bad driver even if you aren't driving badly. The Netradyne system is productive not just representative; by generating abstract metrics like 'Following Distance events' and by applying the consequent penalties, it produces both 'safety' and 'bad drivers', even if they don't directly correspond to entities we'd have previously labelled as such.

The Amazon/Netradyne system is an example of performativity. The term 'performativity' refers to the mode of producing that which it is claimed is simply being described. In the example of Amazon's driver surveillance, the system is not simply recording bad driving but constructing a set of parameters to redefine the notion of bad driving in its own terms. In general, applied algorithms are performative in that they help to reshape the very phenomenon they are supposedly modelling. In the late 1970s, for example, the addition of sophisticated computer modelling to financial futures trading had the effect of altering trading behaviour to fit in with the assumptions of the model (Mackenzie, 2008). The new algorithmic reasoning was too complex to be challenged by traders, who, as a consequence, abandoned some of their previous intuitions about markets and took to gaming the new mathematical proxies, which had become dominant because all the other traders were using them as well. The market became what the algorithm said it was, even though the algorithm didn't capture attributes that had been previously observed and acted on by the traders. Machine learning's performativity will be amplified through feedback because its interventions will change the very data distributions that it learns from.

Performativity also applies to social relationality. We tend to think of gender, for example, as innate and given, but it can perhaps be better understood as inscribed by the actions of its repeated performance (Butler, 2011). Bodies, clothing and behaviours form a generally self-reinforcing categorization of what is masculine and what is feminine, which is not solid and inflexible but subject to overlap, blur and change. The sense of stability comes from repetitive reiteration, which means that changes can emerge from different performativities. If AI has access to data about even the smallest interactions in our lives, it has the potential to affect these more intimate kinds of performativity. AI's granular interventions at the level of everyday life will interact with the forms of performativity that already underpin our deeper sense of subjectivity and embodied being, for example, of our sense of being 'attractive', 'trustworthy' or 'hardworking'. As the iterative channelling of daily life according to the solution-oriented predictions of algorithms expands into our intersubjective experiences, it will alter our sense of how we should act in order to be who we are.

The problem with AI's approach to solving problems is not only its performativity but the way it obscures the possibility of a structural break with the past. Even when it seems to produce 'new' knowledge it is doing so in a way that is wholly tied to the conditions under which the training data was generated. This looking back not only applies to the training data but to AI's mode of analysis, which is based on 'resemblances ... between the new object which we are studying and others which we believe we already know' (Bergson, 1999, cited in Coleman, 2008). So whatever problem AI attempts to solve becomes what philosopher Henri Bergson would call a 'ready-made problem' – a problem that is expressed as a function of things prior to itself that have already been turned into abstractions.

Bergson argued that if one accepts a ready-made problem in this way,

> one might just as well say that all truth is already virtually known, that its model is patented in the administrative offices of the state, and that philosophy is a jig-saw puzzle where the problem is to construct with the pieces society gives us the design it is unwilling to show us. (Deleuze, 2002, cited in Coleman, 2008)

In other words, however sophisticated or creative AI might seem to be, its modelling is stuck in abstractions drawn from the past, and so becomes a rearrangement of the way things have been rather than a reimagining of the way things could be. AI has, in effect, an inbuilt political commitment to the status quo, in particular to existing structures that embed specific relations of power. The absence of different concepts leaves out the possibility of conceiving that things could be arranged differently.

This innate conservatism makes AI a good fit with the broader tendency in contemporary society known as 'tech solutionism' – the substitution of advanced technology for any serious attempt to address the structural causes of a problem. Tech solutionism looks for what tech might be to hand rather than what injustices need to be addressed. It was on full display during the early stages of the COVID-19 pandemic, when enthusiasm for Bluetooth proximity tracking was seen as preferable to an epidemiological response that took into account existing social inequities, such as the need to pay low-waged workers on zero-hours contracts to stay home and isolate where necessary. As AI scales its machinic solutions to ready-made problems, it will become the vanguard of wider tech solutionism.

The belief that the pattern-finding technology of AI can be a solution to pretty much any problem is exacerbated by its apparent generalizability between domains. So, for example, deep learning models developed for natural language translation are used to 'translate' between pharmaceutical drugs and the metabolites that they produce in the human liver (Litsa et al, 2020), and this kind of approach is applied to existing datasets as a way of generating potential candidates for new medication. The opaque layers of probabilistic pattern matching inside deep learning are taken as a kind of 'intuition machine' that can be applied across a potentially limitless range of activities. Despite the brittleness of AI and the harms it can cause, there's a heady sense that AI will soon replace people in all sorts of cognitive and relational tasks, and furthermore that this is what we need to solve our various overlapping crises.

One feature of this belief system is its ability to weather empirical evidence to the contrary. When a UK startup called Babylon Health claimed that its diagnostic AI outperformed the average human doctor, it turned out that not only were the claims distorted and manipulated (Fraser and Wong, 2018) but in fact there was evidence of the app giving inaccurate, unsafe and dangerous advice to patients (Hsu, 2019). Nevertheless, Babylon Health continued to garner very public support from the government's minister of health (Clarke, 2018) while continuing to cherry-pick profitable patients from a cash-starved NHS (Burgess and Kobie, 2019). Society is being subsumed in what we might call, after Mark Fisher's concept of Capitalist Realism, an atmosphere of 'AI Realism'. Fisher observed that the somewhat paradoxical response to the financial crash of

2007–08 was not a widespread questioning of the capitalist system but a more entrenched belief in it. Capitalist Realism refers to a 'widespread sense that not only is capitalism the only viable political and economic system, but also that it is now impossible even to imagine a coherent alternative to it' (Fisher, 2009). The fact that AI solutions don't live up to the hype is overridden by AI Realism's sense of inevitability.

The effect of AI solutionism won't simply be the emergence of one misperforming system after another but an overall shift in society's direction of travel. AI is a technology of anticipation and pre-emption, and its discrimination operates not only in the here and now but as a way of discriminating between different possible futures. The goal of AI is to intervene on the basis of predicted risk, so applied AI becomes an anticipatory system that, seeing a particular future, pre-empts it. It's one thing if this is being applied to the movements of a robot arm where the risk is of dropping an object, but another when the AI is making a determination about the sharing out of life chances. The net effect of pre-emption is to bring a particular future into the present (Massumi, 2016): it makes real the future that it predicted in order to act on it in the here and now. AI's solutionism selects some futures while making others impossible to even imagine. The question remains as to who's future it will be selecting for.

This chapter has reviewed the trajectory that AI follows as it travels between being a set of technical operations and being seen as a social solution. We have looked at the way the brittleness of AI generates the potential for harm that exceeds technical or ethical checks, at the way this manifests as discrimination and injustice despite attempts at legal regulation, and at the way this becomes embedded when AI is applied as a solutionism. In the field of AI, the activity of checking the models and data for possible bias or adverse outcomes is known as auditing: one implication of this chapter is that that what really needs auditing is our existing social structures. The way AI constructs problems to be solved diverts our attention from the underlying issues, thereby enabling the extractivism of the status quo to continue unabated. In the process it reconstructs us as subjects who can be blamed as the source of those same problems. In the next chapter we will see how this tainted solutionism plays out as part of structures at the level of society as a whole, in particular within the frameworks of science, work, bureaucracy and race. It turns out that solutionism at scale not only diverts from alternatives but provides new channels for social exclusion. We will see that applying AI's abstractions to the institutional status quo has the effect of intensifying structural violence.

3

AI Violence

Artificial intelligence is not some kind of science fiction reality that takes us seamlessly into a new era. As we saw in Chapter 2, AI is not a clean break from what came before but continues forms of ordering that reinforce the status quo. In this chapter we'll look at what happens when AI becomes entangled with existing institutional systems and how the net effect of this is increased bureaucratic thoughtlessness and general precarity. We'll start by looking at the way AI poaches its legitimacy from science, as its association with the superiority of scientific ways of knowing plays a major role in diverting attention from its actual impact in intensifying structural violence.

Scientism

When we're talking about the authority and cultural power of AI, we need to talk about science, especially about the ways AI is and isn't like it. AI emulates science by collecting data and making models, but the predictions of AI diverge from scientific process; they are not the expressions of a hypothesis, a coherent theory about the way things work, but simply extrapolations from superficial patterns. There's no cumulative support for an AI model from other non-falsified hypotheses that accumulate into a working understanding of the world. Unlike a scientific theory, machine learning isn't trying to model the actual dynamics of a system, it is simply trying to make probabilistic predictions. Statistics is used by AI, as it is by science, but not in a way that tells us how much confidence we can have in our choice of parameters or whether they're a good description for the underlying process. AI is not realist but instrumentalist: it only models the world to get something out of it.

However, AI imitates science in its approach to legitimizing its results. AI is not simply a method but an organizing idea – a framework that is used to make sense of the world in a particular way. Philosopher of science Thomas Kuhn called this kind of organizing idea a paradigm: a persistent underlying framework of understanding that acts as a kind of container for specific theories and practices (Kuhn, 1996). A paradigm provides a widely diffused logic that other specific ideas and solutions need to fit within if they are to 'make sense'. A paradigm persists even in the face of contradictory evidence, until it is replaced by a different paradigm. AI makes sense not only because it can carry out specific tasks but because it's being promoted as a paradigm – as a general way to develop an understanding of the world.

AI is trying to prove its worth as a paradigm in the same way that science had to. Science established itself by showing that mathematical representations of the world could supersede the predictions of our senses by providing an explanation for phenomena from the relative movement of the planets and the Sun (Copernicus) to the motion of bodies on the Earth's surface (Galileo). Science overturned both medieval scholasticism and everyday intuition to assert itself as the most reliable method of explaining the world. AI tries to emulate science by revealing a hidden mathematical order in the world that is superior to our direct experience. The optimizations of AI, it is claimed, can find patterns faster than we can or, indeed, that escape us entirely, and it does so through the datafication of the world. Therefore, we should have confidence in AI as something that can enhance, or even replace, human activity in applications as diverse as medical care or child protection.

We saw plenty of reasons in the previous chapter why we shouldn't have this blind confidence in AI. However, we'll spend a few paragraphs here digging into the underlying characteristics that AI has borrowed from science, as they have a major role in producing and justifying the social impacts described in the rest of the chapter. In particular we'll look at AI's operations of abstraction, reduction and representation, and how they construct a viewpoint that can claim to be 'objective' and 'neutral' while being deployed in the interests of the powerful against the needs of the powerless.

Abstraction is core to the scientific method. In order to render the world as part of a theory, that is, in the form of equations, science had to differentiate between primary qualities that could be quantified and secondary qualities that were seen as mere sensory side effects. When Newton explained refraction, for example, he replaced colour with a number (the 'degree of refrangibility'). In a similar way, the operations of AI depend on datafication: the presentation of the world as data separated out from the continuity of experience. Unfortunately, one corollary of abstraction is the effect that philosopher of science Alfred North Whitehead criticized as 'explaining away': by treating abstractions as something concrete, everything that does not fit into the schema is denied the status of proper existence (Whitehead, 1997). The error comes from treating abstractions as more real than phenomena. This kind of reified abstraction is a key mechanism of instrumental rationalities like AI – the trick that allows it to see only that which can be made useful and ignore the rest.

AI's abstractions are reductionist; they provide a description of reality in terms of an already limited set of features, which are then reduced even further through the internal transformations of deep learning. AI misrepresents this reductiveness as objectivity, despite all the evidence we've seen so far that it is anything but objective. On one level, AI's reductiveness is a mathematical phenomenon of transforming and compressing the data until it is distilled into the required output classes. On another level, however, AI takes on the kind of reductiveness that was described by the philosopher Heidegger; that is, a reduction of being itself (Chun, 2009).

Heidegger used the idea of 'enframing' to describe how technology shapes the way the world is revealed – the way it is seen and understood. According to Heidegger, the enframing of modern science and technology, the all-encompassing way in which the world is revealed under this calculative ordering, is as a standing reserve. That is, a mountain is not a mountain in itself but a standing reserve of coal to be mined; a river is not the flowing water in itself but a standing reserve of hydro-electric power. From this perspective, anything subject to AI's enframing is reduced to a calculative order, which drives out every other possibility of revealing (Heidegger and Lovitt, 1977) – that is, it removes any other way to see or understand the subject. Converting the social world into data for the benefit of AI is to convert ourselves into a standing reserve for optimization and prediction. We are abstracted and reduced to that which can be usefully optimized.

AI operationalizes this reductive view through its representations. As explained in Chapter 1, AI's representations of the world consist of the set of weights in the layers plus the model architecture of the layers themselves. Like science, AI's representations are presented as distinct from that which they claim to represent. In other words, there is assumed to be an underlying base reality that is independent of the practices by which such representations are constructed. But, as we saw in Chapter 2, the entities represented by AI systems – the 'careful Amazon driver' or the 'trustworthy citizen' – are partly constructed by the systems that represent them. AI needs to be understood not as an instrument of scientific measurement but as an apparatus that establishes 'relations of becoming' between subjects and representations. The subject co-emerges along with the representation. The society represented by AI is the one that it actively produces.

Overall, AI perpetuates the 'view from nowhere'. The view from nowhere is the claim to a neutral and disinterested view of the world. Science itself is the ultimate expression of this viewpoint: the scientific observer is a 'modest witness' (Haraway, 1997) who allows nothing subjective to interfere with the construction and observation of the experiment and the recording of the results. Scientific experiments are deemed to provide an objective conception of nature as the basis for explaining, predicting and controlling phenomena (Reiss and Sprenger, 2020). The scientific viewpoint is one that AI also tries to lay claim to: by absorbing the raw data from a particular context and applying the optimizations of computation, it too can rise above any particular set of interests to produce objective insights.

AI is a form of scientism. It uses the aura of science to perpetuate the idea that its abstract mathematical models provide a reliable way of knowing, and promotes a reductive definition of truth that is claimed as inherently superior to lived experience. The scientism of AI allows alternative perspectives to be blunted or dismissed as subjective, and it reinforces the notion of representations that stand outside and above the context which they are used to pronounce judgement on. But, in practice, AI acts as an epistemic power grab that conceals politics and ideology under its machinic opacity. As we'll see later in this chapter, and in the next, the invocation of science-like authority provides AI with the cover to propagate a variety of different forms of violence.

Precarity

Having looked at the way AI tries to establish its legitimacy through abstraction, we now turn our attention to the effects of AI's systemic and institutional application. AI as we know it has flourished under neoliberalism, a political-economic order which establishes markets and individuals as the constituent elements of society, and the globalization of free trade and supply chains as the mode of production. These structures already depend on datafication – on the rendering of the material world as elements that can be manipulated and optimized, whether that's via container shipping or consumer preferences. This datafication also makes the world readily available to the operations of AI, and what we're interested in here is which characteristics of the neoliberal system are amplified as a result of the use of AI.

In the Global North, one of the main impacts of neoliberalism has been deindustrialization, with a shift to service jobs based on temporary contracts and casualized labour, and a loss of rights at work, which has gone hand-in-hand with the hollowing out of welfare support. The label for this general condition of fragility is 'precarity', a condition which leaves people open to greater exploitation and increases their vulnerability. Precarity captures, in a single term, aspects of both the worsening conditions in the Global North and the ongoing immiseration of life in the Global

South. Let's not forget that austerity measures began well before the financial crash of 2008, and the International Monetary Fund (IMF) has been imposing austerity programmes on the Global South since the 1970s. As we will see shortly, the operations of AI make it a good fit for neoliberalism's retreat from social care and unrelenting hostility to organized labour. While AI is a technology that claims to calculate risk and therefore reduce uncertainty, it actually acts to increase precarity. Applied AI is not so much a means of prediction as an engine of precaritization.

AI also amplifies precariousness on an ecological level. Data centres increasingly consume scarce water resources in regions already impacted by global warming (Solon, 2021), while the water 'becomes a repository for electronic waste and derivative toxins, making toxicity a permanent feature of surrounding systems and ecologies' (Dryer, 2021). Despite greenwashing announcements about reduced carbon emissions and 'Green AI', the thrust of AI continues with 'economic growth agendas that harm the environment in many other ways (e.g., pursuing lucrative contracts with oil and gas companies)' (Dryer, 2021). And indeed, Amazon aggressively markets its AI to the oil and gas industry with programmes like 'Predicting the Next Oil Field in Seconds with Machine Learning' while Microsoft holds events such as 'Empowering Oil & Gas with AI' (Dobbe and Whittaker, 2019). Despite bandying about the idea that AI is a key part of the solution to the climate crisis, the real modus operandi of the AI industry is its offer to accelerate and optimize fossil fuel extraction and climate precarity.

Returning to the topic of precarious work, the kind of platform labour that is enabled by algorithms and AI is strongly reminiscent of the home-based piecework and 'putting out' that were central to nineteenth-century industrial production. Abstract optimization, it seems, becomes a means of heightened exploitation. Platforms like Uber give access to human capacities but as decomposed and standardized elements in large algorithmic assemblages with AI at their heart. All the risk in these arrangements is transferred to the individual, whether it's unpaid time spent waiting around for a ride or a delivery, the wear and tear on vehicles, or the psychological stress. From Deliveroo in Europe to Meituan in China, delivery riders pushing themselves to satisfy the optimizations of an algorithm are paying the price in terms of exhaustion, injury and fatal accidents (Jones, 2020; Youxuan, 2020). Platform work, online or offline, comes without the protections, such as sick pay, holiday entitlement, pensions or health and safety, that were hard won by the historical struggles of organized labour. As well as the decomposition of individual subjectivity, there's a fragmentation of the kind of community and solidarity that has historically empowered resistance through strikes and other industrial actions (Berardi, 2011, p 101). AI is a futuristic technology that helps to push back the conditions of work by a century or more.

The precaritizing effects of algorithmic labour are made possible by Orwellian levels of data capture. Algorithms instill a disciplinary modulation of workers' behaviour, whether that's the threat of automated firing hanging over Amazon warehouse workers or the myriad of behaviour thresholds hemming in Uber drivers, from acceleration patterns to music levels in the car to attitude towards riders (Jamil, 2020). This can lead to continuous anxiety and constant self-adaptation, to the extent that some Uber drivers, for example, use dashcams to document their own performance of non-adversarial behaviours. The fear of a privileged algorithmic observer leads to an anxious performance of compliance.

The so-called optimization of the work is effected by a reduction of the worker's embodied or emotional being. The efficiency of the Amazon warehouse leads to high levels of musculoskeletal disorder because of the bodily stress of repetitive motion without variation or respite (Evans, 2019). The job of a 'rebinner', for example, is to take an item off a conveyor belt, press a button, put the item in whatever storage bin the monitor screen has instructed, then press another button and repeat the whole cycle. One 'rebinner' compared the work 'to doing a twisting lunge every 10 seconds, nonstop' while being 'encouraged to move even faster by a giant leaderboard, featuring a cartoon sprinting man, that showed the rates of the 10 fastest workers in real time' (Dzieza, 2020b). Any tiny moments of potential relief, which the worker characterized as 'micro rests' (Dzieza, 2020b), were continually optimized out of the system. The same kind of gruelling and relentless elimination of moments of recovery is applied to algorithmically driven social interactions. In insurance industry call centres, for example, the automation of routine call handling by AI-powered chatbots means that workers only get passed the difficult and potentially more traumatic calls, leading to the algorithmic amplification of their emotional labour and stress.

The scale of AI operations behind these precaritizing platforms is truly spectacular, with Uber's routing engine dealing with 500,000 requests and hundreds of thousands of GPS points per second (Uber Engineering, 2018). Watching videos about these feats of engineering, it's impossible not to be struck by the irony that such magnificent achievements are directed largely at the immiseration of ordinary workers. A further irony is that the aim of much of the data capture and algorithmic optimization is to further precaritize their conditions, hence the use of Uber's data in its attempt to develop self-driving cars, and Amazon's use of data to increase the robotization of its warehouses: thanks to the affordances of AI, the data treadmill not only maximizes extraction of value from each worker but uses that same activity to threaten their replacement.

Speculation

Another level on which datafication and AI operate as mechanisms of instability is financialization. Captured data, and the computational systems able to exploit it, attract venture capital and financial valuation in anticipation of further efficiencies, or even an eventual monopoly of full automation. The data becomes an asset class with both use value and speculative financial value (van Doorn and Badger, 2020). The feedback loop of machine learning means that each new adaptation by workers to self-optimize under precarious conditions becomes absorbed into the next model, which is then advertised as a rationale for the next round of funding. The data derivatives become forms of financialized asset in themselves, dependent on a continual ramping up of exploitation and expropriation as a form of performance for investors.

As well as being the motor of the platform economy, AI contributes to precarity more widely by spreading the social logic of this financial speculation into the rest of life. We can see how this works by comparing the operations of AI with the operations of financial derivatives. Derivatives are forms of asset based on unbundled attributes of concrete reality, made into tradeable packages that combine complex bets about rising and falling prices at specific points in time. While they started out as data related to the pricing of traditional commodities like US grain or Saudi oil, they are as likely these days to be derived from aspects of the weather, sports performance or health insurance. Derivatives are a way of repackaging abstractions to provide a contractual foundation for financial speculation.

Like AI, the derivatives market bets on correlations not on causations. Speculative trading requires a minimum level of commensurability: for a market to be possible there needs to be a way to compare the value of very different kinds of things. The financial derivatives market is not about trading bets on oil prices for bets on oil prices, or even health insurance debts for health insurance debts, but packages that mix data about these and other unrelated aspects of the world. In the derivatives market, this comparability comes from the Black–Scholes equation, which uses partial differential equations to standardize the future volatility of an asset. In AI, a similar commensurability is made possible by the differential equations of backpropagation and the way stochastic gradient descent trades different kinds of data against each other during optimization.

With this commensurability in place, the financial markets are free to create their dizzying casinos of speculative trading. It should be no surprise, then, if AI carries forward into everyday life what sociologist Randy Martin called the social logic of the derivative (Martin, 2013, cited in Arvidsson, 2016) – a logic of fragmentation, financialization and speculation. This is a precaritizing logic that depends on the decomposition of that which was previously whole (the job, the asset, the individual life) so that operations can be moved into a space that's free of burdensome attachments to the underlying entity, whether that's the fluctuating price of actual commodities or the frailty of the actual worker.

As AI expands into more areas of activity through infrastructure, commerce and statutory services, it opens up channels for speculation and precaritization to flow deeper into previously unquantified and untradeable dimensions of living. The data assets to be gambled with will be matters of individual and social concern, from mental health to immigration, and the derived risks will be packaged into representations of institutional and state interests. It's instructive to note that financial derivatives are not really a mechanism for eliminating risk. Prices must move up and down so money can be made by betting on those changes; derivatives depend on wider volatility to extract value. Likewise, the prospect of pervasive algorithmic prediction across fields of social interaction is not the elimination of social risk but the creation of a fluctuating market in citizen futures. There is no correlation that can't become a form of speculation.

The centring of correlation as a strategy of ordering will also have precaritizing psychosocial consequences. Machine learning already contributes to an atmosphere of paranoia through its role in social media, where AI-driven recommendation algorithms optimize engagement by amplifying various popular conspiracies, many of which are gateways to involvement in far-right politics. Beyond social media, AI proliferates non-causal connections via its ever-expanding circles of data collection, producing unchallengeable judgements through its innate opacity. Its connectionism drives a kind of apophenia, 'the perception of connectedness in unrelated phenomena', along with 'a sense of abnormal meaningfulness' (Brugger, 2001), while it applies a veneer of suspicion to these connections through the elevation of risk as the primary metric. Thus, the deeper relationship of AI to paranoia comes from AI itself exhibiting key features of a conspiracy theory.

The realm of algorithmic social order may bear more resemblance than we'd care to admit to the experiences described in Kafka's *The Trial* (Kafka, 2010). In that tale, the main character is prosecuted by a remote authority without the nature of his supposed crime ever being revealed. The parallels with speculative AI are not only in a form of life that is interrupted by mysterious interventions but also because of the psychological rendings that we, like *The Trial*'s suspect Joseph K., may inflict on ourselves as a response. While the frame of Kafka's tale is the matter-of-fact surrealness of his arrest and arraignment, a large part of the text is the protagonist's almost sadomasochistic response to the way the trial redefines his relationships and social status. We should be asking how our mental models of normal relations between ourselves, others and institutions will be distorted if subjected to apparently baseless interventions stamped with the authority of calculative objectivity. Joseph K.'s world erupts with events and structures dislocated from their familiar settings, like the mysterious court room nested within the dank corridors of a deprived housing estate. Pervasive AI will, in turn, displace judgement from its familiar locations in specific discourse and structures and spread it into the micro-interactions of daily life.

System risk

Having looked at the way AI is precaritizing both work and life beyond work, we turn our attention to the way this precarity and speculation becomes instantiated in the welfare state. While the most visible and attention-grabbing applications of AI are innovations like self-driving cars, some of its most far-reaching impacts will be through its background adoption by bureaucratic systems. We will consider here how the abstractions of AI will amplify the mundane violence of the welfare systems that claim to be society's safety net.

The feedback loop between algorithmic amplification and bureaucratic discrimination is already a strong one. In Sweden, for example, an algorithmic system is already issuing warnings about 'suspicious' benefit claims and was found to have wrongly withheld benefit payments from thousands of people (Wills, 2019). In Spain, an algorithmic system for processing electricity subsidies turned out to have been discarding applications from poor households (Kayser-Bril, 2019). In Austria, an algorithmic system used to classify job seekers for additional support was shown to discriminate against applicants based on gender and disability (Kayser-Bril, 2019). Most of these systems are clumsy codifications of paper-based systems, whose automated injustices have been uncovered by vigilant journalists and civil society observers. Nevertheless, they show both the way that public institutions are seeking to apply tech solutionism, and the way that such 'solutions' will incorporate existing prejudices. To dig a bit deeper, we'll look at two examples where algorithmic decision-making is already making inroads into local and national governance, and how the results presage the likely impacts of full AI.

In the Netherlands, an algorithm called SyRI (Systeem Risico Indicatie, or System Risk Indication) tapped into a large array of government databases to draw up lists of people suspected of housing or benefits fraud by calculating their similarity to data profiles of previous fraudulent claims. SyRI cast a very wide net, drawing in data not just about tax, health insurance, naturalization and debt, but potentially data points like water bills and rubbish collection which might indicate a different household occupancy than the one qualifying for a benefit payment. The perspective behind SyRI was of the 'beneficiary as a shrewd scammer, constantly looking for loopholes' (Bij Voorbaat Verdacht, 2020), rather than someone in need who might be misrepresented by the available data. SyRI was applied to neighbourhoods with high levels of poverty and deprivation and, when the algorithm was configured, the data analyst set parameters that defined the local 'risk range'. So not only was the algorithm being applied as a form of ghettoization, the specifics of its impacts were being tuned by an engineer rather than being subject to democratic oversight.

SyRI is an example of the way policy-making can be subsumed into data science while at the same time targeting stigmatized communities, who are assumed to consist of 'multi-problem families' marked by the 'erosion of values and norms' (Braun, 2018). The next step in this invisible shift to algorithmic governance of the public will be the replacement of current systems by machine learning and AI. These technologies offer exactly what under-pressure bureaucracies are required to deliver in terms of management by metrics and the ruthless optimization of outcomes. In the UK, the High Court ruled that the government could justify a discriminatory benefits systems based on automated decision-making as legitimate, in this case a system that determined COVID-19 income support for self-employed women who had been on maternity leave, because the discriminatory algorithm was 'quicker, cheaper and ... more straight-forward' than alternatives (Allen QC and

Masters, 2021). AI will increase both the scope of operations that can be delegated to algorithmic systems and the opportunity for unaccountable 'policy by hyperparameter'. In effect, AI becomes the scaling of structural violence – the form of violence by which institutions or social structures harm people through preventing them from meeting their fundamental needs (Galtung, 1969).

Another prehension of bureaucratic AI is provided by the Australian government's 'robodebt' program. Powered by a simple algorithm, this system issued hundreds of thousands of erroneous debt notices to welfare recipients. The system averaged a person's income over the year, defining welfare as 'overpayments' even for periods where people with fluctuating incomes had literally no other money coming in (Easton, 2017), and issued automated repayment demands based on these miscalculations. A significant feature of robodebt was the way due process was inverted to place the legal burden of proof on the welfare recipient. Its calculation was treated as fact in law, and the alleged debtor was told to pay up unless they could provide exact paperwork, going back up to seven years, proving that the demand was in error (Easton, 2019). Its demands were passed to privatized debt collection agencies, which were paid on commission (Towell, 2017) and, unsurprisingly, resorted to threats (Revanche, 2018). The algorithm was weaponized by its fusion with the law and the mechanisms of enforcement.

It was only after a sustained campaign, which reverse engineered the calculations, tracked and exposed the scale of the problem, and mobilized a broad coalition of collective opposition, that the government was reluctantly forced to admit that the algorithm was itself unlawful. 'Robodebt was bureaucratic violence enabled by lack of government accountability. Its prime purpose was the dogmatic pursuit of a campaign of cruelty against the unemployed, disabled people, single parents, care-givers, casual and gig economy workers' (Wolf, 2020). Even after the campaign and successful legal challenge, the government department responsible refused to apologize, either for the wrongful debt demands or for the toll of distress, panic and additional hardship. Provided with political shielding by a right-wing government, robodebt is an illustration of ideological commitment to algorithmic cruelty at scale.

Administrative violence

Rather than heralding an alternative sci-fi future, AI can be more plausibly understood as an upgrade to the existing bureaucratic order. The affordances of AI make it a good fit with the bureaucratic logic that shapes both governments and corporations, and it is as bureaucratic ordering that some of the discriminatory impacts of AI will be most keenly felt. The merging of bureaucracy and AI is really a kind of continuity, as the discipline of statistics has been wedded to the needs of the state from its very inception. Bureaucracy, according to its most well-known theorist Max Weber, emerged as a mechanism for the state to impose control and rationality on increasingly complex societies, and AI is part of the same quest for traction on an increasingly complex and turbulent world. AI's predictions are the latest version of 'seeing like a state' (Scott, 1999).

Like AI, bureaucracy is a generalized and goal-oriented mode of rational ordering which lays claim to neutrality and objectivity. It is also justified by the idea of efficiency at scale and, like AI, introduces a fundamental opacity as part of that scaling. Even Weber himself observed that 'bureaucratic administration always tends to exclude the public, to hide its knowledge and action from criticism as well as it can' (Weber, 1978, p 992). Like AI, the architecture of bureaucracy deals with the world through abstract categories and the construction of distance. Bureaucracy abstracts from the detail of social life in order to extend 'the distance at which human action is able to bring effect' (Bauman, 1989, p 194). Weber interpreted the bureaucratic approach not only as a matter of organization but as a matter of moral comportment, one that valorizes indifference as the means to effective implementation of policy. However, as we'll see in this section, it's through distancing and indifference that AI amplifies the most harmful behaviours of the bureaucratic state.

One consequence of the bureaucratic nature of AI will be the scaling of what philosopher Miranda Fricker refers to as epistemic injustice. This is a term she developed through analyzing the historical disempowerment of women when it came to challenging harassment and abuse, and refers in general to the way people are rendered unable to challenge injustice. One kind of epistemic injustice is testimonial injustice, where prejudices cause people to 'give a deflated level of credibility to a speaker's word' (Fricker, 2007, p 1). It's easy to see how this might apply where the assessment of an expert algorithm conflicts with the testimony of an already marginalized welfare applicant. The other kind of epistemic injustice is hermeneutical injustice, 'a kind of injustice in which someone is wronged specifically in her capacity as a knower' (Fricker, 2007, p 20). Fricker points to this as the kind of injustice experienced by social groups who lack the resources to make sense of their own experience. AI contributes to hermeneutical injustice because the complexity and opacity of AI-driven interventions are inherent barriers to any independent effort at comparable sense-making (van den Hoven, 2019).

Even where a 'data subject' can get hold of his or her data, as Deliveroo riders did via data protection legislation after the platform's algorithm falsely terminated them for fraud (van Doorn and Badger, 2020), it tells them very little about how the system will judge them in relation to opaque correlations abstracted from data about thousands of other people. The widespread application of machine learning points to a growth in learned helplessness among data subjects, who are unable to comprehend the decisions that are being made, unable to discuss them meaningfully with others and unable to effectively dispute them, thus dispensing with the core characteristics of due process and democratic accountability.

AI's epistemic injustice overlays already existing cultural and institutional systems of superiority. The marriage of bureaucratic paternalism and epistemically superior AI was perfectly captured by the UK's Head of Transformation for Troubled Families who, while acknowledging that predictive analytics might be 'confusing being poor with poor parenting' and might be flagging the disadvantaged simply because there's more data about them, proceeded to dismiss any challenge to the new technologies as 'protectionism' (Selwyn, 2018). Epistemic violence is a term used by post-colonial theorists to describe the way the experiences of people in former colonies only become known through knowledge created by the distant colonial centre, in a process that constitutes them as the inferior and problematic Other (Spivak, 1988). Where algorithmic knowledge claims increase marginalization, they become a form of epistemic violence.

As we've already seen, most institutional applications of AI won't completely remove the human from the loop. However, few staff are likely to have deep technical insight into the workings of machine learning systems and, especially in times of austerity, they are likely to be working in contexts where everyone is already over-stretched and stressed. Under these conditions, AI will produce the kind of thoughtlessness that Hannah Arendt warned us about (Arendt, 2006). Thoughtlessness manifests as the inability to critique instructions, the lack of reflection on consequences, and a commitment to the belief that the correct ordering is being carried out. It is the psychopolitical product of a certain kind of apparatus − of a certain arrangement of ways of knowing, cultural values and institutional arrangements. Thoughtlessness enables participants to evade any responsibility for wider harms.

Of course, thoughtlessness has always been one of the side effects of bureaucracy. Bureaucratic abstraction puts distance between the functionary and the consequences of their actions. Where tasks are separated so that each merely carries out their part within the overriding logic of the administrative machine, people are able to disengage from the bigger picture in terms of their part in the final outcomes. AI amplifies this by adding computational opacity and technical authority. The way AI weighs things in the balance depends on interlocking influences that are often distant to the point of application, whether that's the latent content of the training data or trade-offs in the optimization of hyperparameters. Arendt also wrote about what she saw as a crisis arising from the split between the knowledge generated by technical ways of knowing and the ability to discuss those truths in normal speech and thought. For Arendt, this also contributed to the generation of thoughtlessness because, if 'knowledge and thought have parted company for good ... we would indeed become the helpless slaves, not so much of our machines as of our know-how, thoughtless creatures at the mercy of every gadget which is technically possible, no matter how murderous it is' (Arendt quoted in Schiff, 2013, p 104).

Arendt developed her concept of thoughtlessness in part from her efforts to comprehend the actions of Nazi war criminal Adolf Eichmann, whose trial she observed at close quarters. She used thoughtlessness to characterize the ability of a functionary in a bureaucratic machine to participate in an ultimately genocidal process. In court, Eichmann was unable to express or explain himself in ways that broke out of bureaucratic jargon: 'Officialese (Amtssprache) is my only language' (Schiff, 2013, p 103). Like many in the SS, he prided himself on his 'objective' attitude. Extermination camps were matters of 'administration', 'economy' and 'solutions'. The conclusion she drew from this extreme case was that thoughtlessness can apply to any systemic arrangement where people are being distanced from acknowledging obvious harms and inhibited from feeling any empathy with those experiencing them. Thoughtlessness can increase suffering by enabling direct acts of deliberate repression or by making it easier to carry out the prosaic oppressions of a punitive welfare system. In institutions with the power to cause social harms, the threat of AI is not the substitution of humans by machines but the computational extension of existing social automatism and thoughtlessness.

The process by which bureaucratic systems coerce people into narrow categories in order to get their needs met, with potentially violent consequences, has been termed 'administrative violence' (Spade, 2015). Sometimes, as with robodebt, these harms are the result of a deliberately punitive policy. In the UK, the routine re-classification of disabled people as 'fit for work', accompanied by the removal of benefits and support, has directly led to a shocking rise in suicide rates (Barr et al, 2016), while JobcentrePlus workers told researchers that top-down pressure to sanction claimants acted as a 'moral anaesthetic', allowing them to use disrespect and psychological harm as a way to reduce the number of people claiming benefits (Redman and Fletcher, 2021). At other times, the harms flow from applying normative categories to fluid identities. The trans community is particularly vulnerable to systems that insist on a single gender choice, especially if that causes a mismatch between record-keeping systems in different institutions. The rise of AI-powered automated gender recognition systems is especially threatening in this regard. An alert from a system triggered by someone apparently being of the 'wrong' gender might lead to a confrontation between a trans person and security or police, an interaction that has every likelihood of ending badly.

Under the bureaucratic gaze, there is little distinction between anomaly and threat. AI didn't create this administrative violence but it will intensify and legitimate it. Its very efficiency drives out the spaces of ambiguity, by means of which people have previously navigated the gap between their particular situations and the demands of institutional order. Its objective function obscures the processes by which social peace can be negotiated. The computations of AI act as a form of cultural violence; that is, a form of culture that makes structural violence look and feel right. This kind of violent social blame, embedded in the repetitions of AI via a kind of machinic innuendo, is exactly the kind of fascization we highlighted in the Introduction.

Racialization

The violence that underpins our social structures has deep historical roots, and its differentiation across race, gender and class reflects that history. AI's presentation as something utterly new, a complete break with what came before, matches the claim of contemporary social systems that they have shed the legacy of empire and slavery. The idea that colonialism ended with the national independence movements of the 1960s ignores the roots of the neoliberal world order and the structuring logics that are carried forward in cultural, political and scientific fields. The wealth distribution and the violence of the contemporary global order continues to be shaped by the historical matrix of plantation, empire and democracy, and this also applies to the global technological order. As much as 'democracy bears the colony within it' (Mbembe and Corcoran, 2019, p 27), then so does deep learning. The global spread of capitalism's hegemony through colonization continues to shape even our most futuristic ventures. The colonial system and the slave system are 'democracy's bitter sediment' (Mbembe and Corcoran,

2019, p 27), and that sediment is being stirred up by advanced computational systems like AI.

If the dark underside of modernity (Ali, 2019) is that its crucible was imperialism then we should be alert to the dark underside of machine learning. AI approaches social problems in a way that obscures their basis in structural violence, extending the way democracies have drawn a veil over their own violent origins. According to decolonial philosopher Frantz Fanon, the democratic order of law is founded in the non-law of its origin, and is dependent on the exteriorization of that originary violence to non-places such as the colony and the camp (Fanon, 1961, cited in Mbembe and Corcoran, 2019). Therefore, an assessment of the meaning of AI means paying close attention to its compatibility with exteriorization and exclusion, and the re-emergence of the segregation of the camp in the form of algorithmic apartheid. These exclusions are not only legacies of the past but prehensions of the coming future. AI is emerging during a fracturing of the dominant neoliberal order, and we are seeing the return of nationalist, authoritarian and fascist logics to mainstream society. AI is not separate from these developments and, as we'll see in Chapter 4, they will bring to the fore the strands of White supremacy latent in the intellectual and cultural framework that AI is built on (Katz, 2020).

Understanding the significance of AI for both capitalist and far-right social formations means appreciating the centrality of racialization. Racialization, the solidifying of differences into a fixed idea of race, was core to the emergence of capitalism as a system: race was used to justify both colonialism and slavery, the 'machine geared toward the elimination of certain classes of human beings located at the interface of the human and the nonhuman, ... the [B]lack as a thing, the burning fossil that fueled capitalism during its primitive era' (Mbembe and Corcoran, 2019). Indeed, proponents of the idea of racial capitalism (Robinson, 2000) argue that racialization is inseparable from capitalism, that the transition from feudalism to capitalism came through colonization inside Europe as well as outside, by processes of settlement, expropriation and racial hierarchy, such that 'the first European proletarians were also racial subjects (Irish, Jews, Roma or Gypsies, Slavs, etc.)' (Kelley, 2017).

AI not only perpetuates racist discrimination but acts, at a deeper level, as a technology of racialization. The only way machine learning knows how to discriminate into output classes is by calculating distances, by determining some abstract metric of difference as a distance. The basis of machine learning is the construction of homophily – statistically induced connections to those who are allegedly 'similar', a forcing of closeness in data space that can be interpreted as a biologized attribute. AI segregates at a data level in the same way that racism itself segregates at a social level (Chun, 2009, cited in Lentin, 2018). Thus, AI lends itself to becoming a racial project, which is 'simultaneously an interpretation, representation, or explanation of racial identities and meanings, and an effort to organize and distribute resources (economic, political, cultural) along particular racial lines' (Omi and Winant, 2014, cited in Hanna et al, 2020).

AI will expand the operation of race by algorithmically diffracting it. We've already seen how AI will sort the distribution of resources and life chances according to statistical classifications, many of which will constitute new kinds of segregation at the level of groups and populations. It will not only reproduce race, gender and class but cross-multiply them with its own optimizing divisions. These optimizations, in turn, nest inside a wider system that relies on social differentiation to define workers as ready for exploitation and the racialized Other as ripe for expropriation (Go, 2021). AI is a racial project that, by assigning different values to parts of populations, will help to 'determine who lives, for how long, and under what conditions' (Spade, 2015). AI acts as racialization because it is ultimately a 'dividing practice' that sustains a 'world of apartness' (Adams, 2021). Moreover, in a fracturing social order inflected by the return of far-right politics, this racialization becomes the naturalization of governance by those understood as being innately superior.

Genetic determinism

It's an ongoing theme of this book that the overall impact of AI results from resonances between its operations and surrounding conditions. One of the concurrent techno-political developments that will reinforce the racializing impacts of AI is the return of deterministic genetics. We'll take a short detour through this field to demonstrate how this works and how the combined result leans even further in the direction of potential fascization.

The racializing and essentializing effects of AI are going to be increasingly compounded by deterministic interpretations of genetics. The way genetic determinism gets expressed reflects the deep entanglement of genetics and computing. It's not just that modern genomics is inseparable from a globalized infrastructure of big data, but that genetics and computation have been understood as similar organizing principles ever since Schroedinger's 1943 lecture 'What is Life?', where he described a genetic 'codescript' as the controlling factor in the living cell (Schrödinger, 1951). The relationship to AI comes through the way that similarly large datasets have been used by interpretations of genetics to reassert biologized notions of race, and through the way that attempts to rescue a deterministic view of genetics have resulted in AI-like predictive systems based on weak correlations. The mantra is that data proves race is real, and that you can predict behaviours from genetic correlations.

The so-called central dogma of genetics was that it programmes our development via an irreversible and one-way flow of information from DNA to proteins to organism. This dogma still persists in some circles despite its substantial replacement in molecular biology by a more complex picture that more or less reverses the roles: the new understanding is that the biochemistry of the cell has more active agency while the DNA is the more passive element. Contemporary science doesn't subscribe to the original picture of the gene as the constant unit of heredity, suggesting instead that genes are transcribed and spliced in different patterns as part of a complex interplay with RNA and proteins. One consequence is that the actual payoff of genomic sequencing has paled in comparison to what was promised in the heady days of the Human Genome Project. While automated sequencing continues to pour genetic data into giant databases at ever-increasing rates, there is little evidence of simple linkages between single genes and conditions or behaviours of interest. But the 'genomic gaze' (Comfort, 2018) of vested interests, of funding structures and their political backers, continues to push for genes-first explanations.

One approach to rescuing the value of this investment is sociogenomics, which dredges databases of genomic information to establish correlations with any social or behavioural phenomena that strikes the researcher as interesting. Sociogenomics gives a hard science gloss to exactly the same kind of predictive correlations as racializing AI. The primary method used within sociogenomics is known as Genome Wide Association Studies, or GWAS (Witte, 2010). The basic idea is that if we can't find strong correlations between single-nucleotide polymorphisms (SNPs) and social behaviours, maybe we can cook something up by adding thousands of very weak correlations. Using data from public repositories and consumer genomics companies like 23andMe, such studies have found patterns of SNPs associated with a dizzying array of traits. The list of results in the UK Biobank includes findings related to cancer and other diseases, patterns apparently associated with depression or anxiety, and also genetic correlations to things such as 'Job involves shift work', 'Time spent driving' and 'Frequency of light DIY in last 4 weeks' (UK Biobank, 2018).

The punchline is that, as with AI, these correlations can be operationalized as risk scores. If it can be asserted that there are correlations between a gene pattern and an observable phenotypic trait, the genome of any individual can be compared to that pattern to generate a 'polygenic risk score' (Dudbridge, 2013), giving an allegedly predictive likelihood of that person developing the trait. Some scientists are keen to cite GWAS as the genetic underpinnings of complex social phenomena, promoting the idea of polygenic report cards that predict risks not only of various diseases but also propensities for future behavior, such as marital fidelity or financial prudence (Comfort, 2018). The thing is, even if there is a hereditary contribution to most aspects of life, the scientific evidence is that environment and culture overwhelm the influence of genetics (Coop, 2018). Genome Wide Association Studies are as much of a pseudoscience as AI's predictions. They don't point to actual causal mechanisms but simply to the possibility of distant correlations that may exist under the certain particular circumstances from which the data was derived, but which equally may evaporate in the light of expanded or alternative data.

This hasn't stopped so-called race realists adopting these results as proof of their supremacist beliefs (Asbury and Plomin, 2013); such studies have been used to bolster the conviction that intelligence is, after all, largely inherited (Lee et al, 2018), and that wasting too much educational resource on people who won't benefit from it is doing everyone a disservice (Young, 2018). Socially predictive genomics are being cited by right-wing pundits in educational and policy circles to justify the striations of race and class. Both the reductiveness of AI and deterministic interpretations of genetics divert attention from social causes of difference. Sociogenomics is the latest manifestation of biological determinism, described by evolutionary biologist Stephen Jay Gould as the proposition that 'the social and economic differences between human groups – primarily races, classes, and sexes – arise from inherited, inborn distinctions and that society, in this sense, is an accurate reflection of biology' (Gould, 1996, p 20). Gould points out that, historically, there's a surge in biological determinism during times of austerity and political instability.

The relative freedom from causality that is common to both sociogenomics and AI leaves an interpretative gap for racist and regressive ideologies to rush in. The biological essentialism of the past merges seamlessly with the data essentialism of the present to provide a way of dodging questions about our political and social structures, and provide us with something else to blame. Deterministic genetics hearkens back to a time when eugenics was seen as a rational form of social governance, and serves as a warning about the potential for AI governance to support supremacist politics.

Race science

The racializing and biologizing potential of AI draws attention to itself through recurrent attempts at physiognomy. Much to the frustration of people concerned with the serious application of machine learning, research papers regularly appear that claim to have found a predictive value between superficial facial features and questionable attributes like criminality. Examples such as 'Automated Inference on Criminality using Face Images' (Wu and Zhang, 2016), based on the AlexNet convolutional neural network we met in Chapter 1, unwittingly reproduce Cesare Lombroso's nineteenth-century project of measurements with calipers and craniographs. Lombroso used his data about the geometries of people's faces and heads to 'prove' that some people were born criminals, conveniently justifying his prejudice that southern Italians were racially inferior to northern Italians (Agüera y Arcas et al, 2017). At roughly the same time as Lombroso was making his measurements, Victorian scientist Francis Galton (who we'll meet again in the next chapter) was pursuing similar goals by superimposing exposures of convicted criminals on the same photographic plate in order to distill out essentially criminal characteristics (Agüera y Arcas et al, 2017). Unfortunately for its advocates, the scientistic character of AI and its immersion in a racist political-economy mean that AI physiognomy is not an anomaly but a symptom of something deeper.

Race science is the mobilization of science-like activity to bolster pre-existing prejudices about race. While being framed in empirical terms, it interprets scientific results to manufacture a scientific foundation for race and racial hierarchy. It does so by claiming the innate superiority of some races and the inferiority of others, thereby justifying differences in social power. One of the reasons it's so hard for AI and genetics to shake off the curse of race science is because it's so deeply entwined with the history of science as a whole. Race science goes right back to the start of scientific classification. When Linnaeus, the creator of the modern taxonomic system, classified the human species he described Europaeus as 'white, serious, strong ... very smart, inventive' and Africanus as 'impassive, lazy. ... Crafty, slow, foolish. ... Ruled by caprice' (Grant, 2019). Race science reappears in tendencies to biologize and essentialize, primarily through genetics but now extending to AI.

Contrary to popular belief, race science didn't disappear after the Second World War, it just went underground. Despite a consensus since the 1950s that race is a social construct, researchers have warned for some time that the narrative of race realism has been making a comeback through the fusion of big data and genetics, especially through discussions about 'populations' that are really a proxy for race (Chow-White and

Green, 2013). Small statistical differences across geographically dispersed groups are interpreted as proving that race has a genetic basis, even though they are swamped by individual variability. Over the decades there have been dedicated networks of people, inside and outside of science, who have been promoting race science, always pushing the idea that there's a 'debate' to be had about the scientific significance of race, and they are finally starting to see their perseverance pay off (Saini, 2019, chapters 4 and 5). While these networks mostly took care to remain under the radar, their beliefs are undergoing a popular resurgence. YouTube videos from the so-called human biodiversity movement, which promotes supposed examples of these genetic group differences, have notched up millions of views (The Wiener Holocaust Library, 2020).

AI's character as a racial project combines with its appeal to scientific authority to make it a candidate mechanism for a modern race science, one that, like the original race science of 1920's USA and 1930's Germany, is intimately entangled with institutional governance. AI is ready-made to operationalize pseudo-science into production-ready systems for the racialist societies of today and tomorrow. AI isn't really a science, but it is ready to become race science.

In this chapter we've seen how scientism is used to legitimize AI's logics of precaritization and speculation, especially as they become part of the institutions of state welfare. However harmful the resulting forms of racialized algorithmic violence may be, they are not the end point of AI's social impacts. In the next chapter we'll chart the entanglement of AI with ongoing forms of societal disintegration, from austerity to far-right politics, as it reveals itself as an apparatus for the production of states of exception.

4

Necropolitics

In Chapter 3 we looked at the ways in which AI is entangled with
our systems of ordering society. In this chapter we'll see how,
under crisis conditions, it helps accelerate a shift towards far-right
politics. AI is emerging from within a convolution of ongoing
crises, each of which has the potential to be fascism-inducing,
including austerity, COVID-19 and climate change. Alongside
these there is an internal crisis in the 'relations of oppression',
especially the general destabilization of White male supremacy
by decolonial, feminist, LGBTQI and other social movements
(Palheta, 2021). The enrolment of AI in the management of
these various crises produces 'states of exception' – forms of
exclusion that render people vulnerable in an absolute sense. The
multiplication of algorithmic states of exception across carceral,
social and healthcare systems makes visible the necropolitics of
AI; that is, its role in deciding who should live and who should
be allowed to die.

Scarcity

From a state point of view, the arguments for adopting AI's
alleged efficiencies at scale become particularly compelling
under conditions of austerity where, in the years following the
financial crash, public administrations have been required to
deal with increased demand while having their resources cut to
the bone. There are more working poor, more children living
below the poverty line, more mental health problems and more
deprivation, but social services and civic authorities have had

their budgets slashed as politicians choose public service cuts over holding financial institutions to account. The hope of those in charge is that algorithmic governance will help square the circle between rising demand and diminished resourcing, and in turn distract attention from the fact that austerity means the diversion of wealth from the poorest to the elites. Under austerity, AI's capacities to rank and classify help to differentiate between 'deserving' and 'undeserving' welfare recipients and enables a data-driven triage of public services. The shift to algorithmic ordering doesn't simply automate the system but alters it, without any democratic debate. As the UN's special rapporteur on extreme poverty and human rights has reported, so-called digital transformation and the shift to algorithmic governance conceals myriad structural changes to the social contract (Alston, 2018). The digital upgrade of the state means a downgraded safety net for the rest of us.

A case in point is the UK Government's 'Transformation Strategy', which was introduced under the cover of the Brexit turmoil in 2017 and set out that 'the inner workings of government itself will be transformed in a push for automation aided by data science and artificial intelligence' (Alston, 2018). The technical and administrative framing allows even token forms of democratic debate to be bypassed, so that 'crucial decisions to go digital have been taken by government ministers without consultation, or even by departmental officials without any significant policy discussions taking place, on the grounds that the move is essentially an administrative matter, rather than involving a potentially game-changing approach to a large swathe of official policy' (Alston, 2019). To narrow down the pool of social benefits claimants, new and intrusive forms of conditionality are introduced that are mediated by digital infrastructures and data analytics. Austerity has already been used as a rationale for ratcheting down social benefits and amplifying the general conditions of precariousness. The addition of automated decision-making adds an algorithmic shock doctrine, where the crisis becomes cover for controversial political shifts that are further obscured by being implemented through code (Klein, 2008).

These changes are forms of social engineering with serious consequences. The restructuring of welfare services in recent years, under a financial imperative of reducing public expenditure, not only generated poverty and precarity but prepared the ground for the devastation of the COVID-19 pandemic, in the same way that years of drought precede the ravages of a forest fire. According to a review by the UCL Institute of Health Equity in the UK (The UCL Institute of Health Equity, 2020), a combination of cutbacks to social and health services, privatization and the poverty-related ill-health of a growing proportion of the population over the decade following the financial crash led directly to the UK having a record level of excess mortality when the pandemic hit. While the sharp end of welfare sanctions are initially applied to those who are seen as living outside the circuits of inclusion, where 'Conditions are imposed on recipients that undermine individual autonomy ... and highly punitive sanctions are able to be imposed on those who step out of line' (Alston, 2019), algorithmically powered changes to the social environment will affect everyone in the long run. The resulting social re-engineering will be marked by AI's signature of abstraction, distancing and optimization, and will increasingly determine how we are able to live, or whether we are able to live at all.

AI will be critical to this restructuring because its operations can scale the necessary divisions and differentiations. AI's core operation of transforming messy complexity into decision boundaries is directly applicable to the inequalities that underpin the capitalist system in general, and austerity in particular. By ignoring our interdependencies and sharpening our differences, AI becomes the automation of former UK prime minister Margaret Thatcher's mantra that 'there is no such thing as society' (Thatcher, 1987). While AI is heralded as a futuristic form of productive technology that will bring abundance for all, its methods of helping to decide who gets what, when, and how are actually forms of rationing. Under austerity, AI becomes machinery for the reproduction of scarcity.

States of exception

AI's facility for exclusion doesn't only extend scarcity but, in doing so, triggers a shift towards states of exception. The general idea of a state of exception has been a part of legal thinking since the Roman empire, which allowed the suspension of the law in times of crisis ('*necessitas legem non habet*' – 'necessity has no law'). It is classically invoked via the declaration of martial law or, in our times, through the creation of legal black holes like that of the Guantanamo Bay detention camp (Steyn, 2004). The modern conception of the state of exception, or *Ausnahmezustand*, was introduced by German philosopher and Nazi Party member Carl Schmitt in the 1920s, who assigned to the sovereign the role of suspending the law in the name of the public good. The state of exception is a paradox because the law is used to invoke a space in which the law literally does not apply. In the previous chapters we've covered some of the ways in which predictive statistical discriminations can prevent data subjects from accessing resources or rights, and does so in ways that evade existing legal protections. In other words, AI has an inbuilt tendency towards creating partial states of exception. AI is not only a technology that is impossible to properly regulate but a mechanism for multiplying exceptions more widely.

A state of exception can't be justified by legal and constitutional power as that's exactly what it nullifies – instead it arises from constituent power, the power by which the legal framework itself is founded. According to philosopher Giorgio Agamben, our norms and rights are themselves rooted in the state of exception because they are constitutional and depend in turn on the constituent power. We are living in a kind of fiction, an existing state of emergency from which we cannot return directly to the state of law 'for at issue now are the very concepts of state and law' (Agamben, 2005, p 87). As liberal regimes deliver decreasing returns, governments and powerful institutions are increasingly turning to states of exception as a solution to their declining legitimacy. These are not the product of dictatorship or tyranny but operate from within apparently liberal and democratic governance. What we need to be alert for, according to Agamben, is not a confusion of legislative and executive powers, in other words not a dictatorship per se, but the separation of law and force of law. Applications of AI fit Agamben's criteria by being able to enforce exclusion while remaining opaque and outside discourse or regulation.

People's lives can be impacted simply by crossing some statistical confidence limit, and they may not even know it. AI's actions of segregating and scarcifying can have the force of the law without being of the law, and will create what we might call 'algorithmic states of exception'.

A prototypical example would be a no-fly list, where people are prevented from boarding planes due to unexplained and unchallengeable security criteria. A leaked US government guide of who should be put on a no-fly list, the March 2013 Watchlisting Guidance (The Intercept, 2014), says 'irrefutable evidence or concrete facts are not necessary' but 'suspicion should be as clear and as fully developed as circumstances permit'. For algorithms, of course, suspicion means correlation. International systems of securitization, such as those implemented by the EU, are increasingly adopting machine learning as part of their mechanics (Statewatch, 2020). What AI systems will add to the logic of the no-fly list are computer-aided suspicions based on statistical correlation, where everyday behaviour can become 'perceived norm deviation' (Abreu, 2014).

It won't be necessary for AI to explicitly construct a state of exception for it to have that effect. An instructive comparison is Poland's so-called 'LGBT-free zones', where, by the middle of 2020, municipalities and regions covering one third of the country had adopted resolutions declaring themselves as being 'pro-family' and free of 'LGBT ideology' (Ciobanu, 2020). Poland's ruling Law and Justice Party has declared LGBT rights an 'imported' ideology, and party officials gave out medals to local politicians who supported the declarations (Noack, 2019), while the Archbishop who compared LGBT people to a 'rainbow plague' (Davis, 2019) was applauded by the Defence Minister. Although largely symbolic in specifically legal terms, the Council of Europe Commissioner for Human Rights stated that, 'Far from being merely words on paper, these declarations and charters directly impact the lives of LGBTI people in Poland' while MEPs condemned the measures as part of 'a broader context of attacks against the LGBTI community in Poland, which include growing hate speech by public and elected officials and public media, as well as attacks and bans on Pride marches and actions such as Rainbow Friday' (Delaleu, 2019). It's not hard to imagine how problematic technologies like AI-powered Automated Gender Recognition could amplify similar forms of chilling effect (Vincent, 2021) through the mutual reinforcement of encoded binaries in the algorithms and the ideological binaries of nationalist, homophobic and misogynist political movements.

Governments are already implementing fully fledged states of exception for refugees and asylum seekers. Agamben uses the term 'bare life' to describe the body under the state of exception, stripped of political or civil existence. This is the life of those condemned to spend time in places like the Moria refugee camp in Greece or the Calais Jungle informal settlement in northern France. Meanwhile, asylum seekers in Italy are coerced into 'hyper-precarious' situations of legalistic non-existence, ineligible for state subsistence (Davies et al, 2017, p 1273). 'The process of legal inclusion – of being nominally documented – in this instance results in de facto exclusion, from the very material objects and political rights that would allow asylum seekers to survive healthily within the EU' (Davies et al, 2017, p 1273). Under the UK's 'Hostile Environment' regime, where 'destitution is built into the asylum system' (Alston, 2018), people with no recourse to public funds due to their immigration status are charged 150 per cent of the actual cost of treatment by the National Health Service, and threatened with deportation if they don't pay the debt (Medien, 2020). Incubated under these conditions, AI states of exception will disseminate 'machine learned cruelty' (Dzodan, 2018) not only at national borders but across the fluctuating boundaries of everyday life.

This diffusion of AI states of exception will come through operations of recursive redlining. Redlining describes the way people in post-war USA were charged more for insurance and healthcare, or denied services or jobs, if they lived in a racially identified part of town. Predictive algorithms will produce new and agile forms of 'personal redlining' (Davidow, 2014) that are dynamic and updated in real-time. The emergence of AI redlining can be seen in examples like Airbnb's AI-powered 'trait analyzer' software, which risk-scores each reservation before it is confirmed. The algorithms scrape and crawl publicly available information such as social media for anti-social and pro-social behaviours, and returns a rating based on a series of predictive models (Blue, 2020).

Users with excellent Airbnb reviews have been banned for 'security reasons', which seem to be triggered by their patterns of friendship and association, although Airbnb refuses to confirm this (Chiel, 2016). The Airbnb patent makes it clear that the score produced by the trait analyzer software is not just based on the individual but on their associations, which are combined into a 'person graph database'. Machine learning combines different weighted factors to achieve the final score, where the personality traits being assessed include 'badness, anti-social tendencies, goodness, conscientiousness, openness, extraversion, agreeableness, neuroticism, narcissism, Machiavellianism, or psychopathy' and the behaviour traits include 'creating a false or misleading online profile, providing false or misleading information to the service provider, involvement with drugs or alcohol, involvement with hate websites or organizations, involvement in sex work, involvement in a crime, involvement in civil litigation, being a known fraudster or scammer, involvement in pornography, or authoring an online content with negative language' (Airbnb, Inc, 2019).

The enrolment of machine learning in punitive redlining is also visible in the case of the NarxCare database. NarxCare is an analytics platform for doctors and pharmacies in the USA to 'instantly and automatically identify a patient's risk of misusing opioids' (Szalavitz, 2021). It's an opaque and unaccountable machine learning system that trawls medical and other records to assign patients an Overdose Risk Score. One classic failing of the system has been misinterpreting medication that people had obtained for sick pets; dogs with medical problems are often prescribed opioids and benzodiazepines, and these veterinary prescriptions are made out in the owner's name. As a result, people with a well-founded need for opioid painkillers for serious conditions like endometriosis have been denied medication by hospitals and by their own doctors. The problems with these systems go even deeper; past experience of sexual abuse has been used as a predictor of likelihood to become addicted to medication, meaning that subsequent denial of medicines becomes a kind of victim blaming. As with so much of socially applied machine learning, the algorithms simply end up identifying people with complex needs, but in a way that amplifies their abandonment. Many states in the USA mandate doctors and pharmacists to use databases like NarxCare under threat of professional sanction, and data about their prescribing patterns is also analyzed by the system, so the deployment of a predictive machine learning system becomes embroiled in a cycle of fear and distrust without redress or due process. A supposed harm reduction system based on algorithmic correlations becomes productive of harmful exclusions.

These kinds of systems are just the start. The impact of algorithmic states of exception will be the mobilization of punitive exclusions based on applying arbitrary social and moral determinations at scale. As AI's partial states of exception become more severe, they will derive their social justification from increased levels of 'securitization'. Securitization is a term used in the field of international relations to label the process by which politicians construct an external threat, allowing the enactment of special measures to deal with the threat. The successful passing of measures that would not normally be socially acceptable comes from the construction of the threat as existential – a threat to the very existence of the society means more or less any response is legitimized. Securitization 'removes the focus on social causation' and 'obscures structural factors' (McKendrick and Finch, 2020); in other words, it operates with the same disdain for real social dynamics as AI itself. The justifications for AI-powered exceptions amount to securitization because, instead of dealing with the structural causes of social crisis, they will present those who fall on the wrong side of their statistical calculations as some kind of existential threat, whether it's to the integrity of the platform or to society as a whole.

Carceral state

One immediate generator of algorithmic states of exception will be predictive policing. Predictive policing exemplifies many aspects of unjust AI that we've covered previously, such as solutionism and structural violence. The perils of deploying algorithms to produce the subjects you expect to see, for example, is very clear in a system like ShotSpotter. ShotSpotter consists of microphones fixed to structures every few city blocks in areas of cities like Chicago, along with algorithms, including AI, that analyze any sounds like loud bangs to determine if they were a gunshot (Stanley, 2021). A human analyst in a central control room makes the final call as to whether to dispatch police to the scene. Of course, the officers in attendance are primed to expect a person who is armed and has just fired a weapon (Laurence, 2021), and the resulting high-tension encounters have been implicated in incidents such as the police killing of 13-year-old Adam Toledo in Chicago's West Side, where body cam footage showed him complying with police instructions just before he was shot dead. ShotSpotter is a vivid example of the sedimentation of inequalities through algorithmic systems, overlaying predictive suspicion onto its deployment in 'predominantly Black and Brown communities' (Laurence, 2021) and resulting, inevitably, in cases of unjust imprisonment (Burke et al, 2021). Other predictive policing systems are more in the classic sci-fi mould of films like 'Minority Report', and are generated by the kind of algorithmic generalization and domain transfer that we looked at in earlier chapters. The widely adopted Predpol system, for example, came out of models of human foraging developed by anthropologists and was turned into a predictive system as part of counterinsurgency efforts in Iraq (Katz, 2020, p 115): it was only later that it was turned to predicting crime in urban areas like Los Angeles.

The conjunction of policing and AI also amplifies the contradictions at the heart of policing itself, as laid out by Walter Benjamin in his 1921 essay 'Critique of Violence' (Benjamin, 2002, p 236). These contradictions are rooted in the same dynamics as the state of exception, in particular the dynamics of law-making and law-preserving. Law-making concerns the constitutive act of establishing power, which is then able to determine the law. Law-preserving describes the nominal role of the police and other state institutions in enforcing the law as it is already laid out. Both depend ultimately on the ability to use violence to achieve these ends: 'All violence as a means is either law-making or law-preserving' (Benjamin, 2005). The constitutive power of law-making is, by definition, also law-destroying because it replaces the law that was previously in place. Benjamin describes the two forms together as 'mythic violence' because they form an inescapable circular logic: 'any law-destroying act results in a new positing (Setzung) of law which again violently tries to preserve itself' (Khatib, 2011). In the practice of policing, and also in predictive policing, these two forms of violence become conflated.

The law as such cannot accommodate all situations, so in order to preserve the law the police are continuously overstepping it. As Benjamin wrote:

> Rather the 'law' of the police really marks the point at which the state, whether from impotence or because of the immanent connections within any legal system, can no longer guarantee through the legal system the empirical ends that it desires at any price to attain. Therefore, the police intervene 'for security reasons' in countless cases where no clear legal situation exists. (Benjamin, 2005, p 243)

Law-making violence is normally derived from an overthrow of the old order, but the police never have to justify their exercise of it; rather, their law-making violence is obfuscated and exempted by the existing legal system. Policing is founded on a form of violence that lies beyond the law. AI adds to this excess of violence by opening up new vistas of pre-crime and predictive suspicion. Acting as it does with a law-like force without being of the law, it merges seamlessly with the way policing operates to continuously exceed the law. Algorithmic predictions are an expansion of this excess under the guise of the law-preserving role of policing. Predictive policing is not simply unjust targeting or an extension of bad policing but an algorithmic frame for an expansion of the violence that constitutes policing per se. Benjamin referred to the fusion of law-preserving and law-making as a 'nowhere-tangible, all-pervasive, ghostly presence' (Benjamin, 2002, p 243) which, in predictive policing, is fused with the equally pervasive apparatus of algorithmic violence.

The cascading effect of securitization and algorithmic states of exception is to expand carcerality, that is, aspects of governance that are prison-like. Carcerality is expanded by AI in both scope and form: its pervasiveness and the vast seas of data on which it feeds extend the reach of carceral effects while the virtual redlining that occurs inside the algorithms reiterates the historical form by fencing people off from services and opportunities. At the same time, AI contributes to physical carcerality through the algorithmic shackling of bodies in workplaces like Amazon warehouses and through the direct enrolment of predictive policing and other technologies of social control in a 'tech to prison pipeline' (Coalition for Critical Technology, 2020). The logic of predictive and pre-emptive methods fuses with the existing focus on individualized notions of crime to extend the attribution of criminality to 'the supposed cultural, biological and cognitive deficiencies of criminalized populations'. These combinations of prediction and essentialism not only provide a legitimation for carceral intervention but also constitute 'the very processes through which these populations are turned into deviants to be controlled and feared' (Coalition for Critical Technology, 2020). AI is carceral not only through its assimilation by the incarcerating agencies of the state but through its innate characteristics. Socially applied AI is ultimately a technology of unfreedom because it closes off possible futures other than those of its own determination.

Necropolitics

The kind of social divisions that are amplified by AI have been put under the spotlight by COVID-19: the pandemic is a stress test for underlying social unfairness. Scarcification, securitization, states of exception and increased carcerality accentuate the structures that already make society brittle, and the increasing polarization of both wealth and mortality under the pandemic became a predictor of post-algorithmic society. It's commonly said that what comes after COVID-19 won't be the same as what came before, that we have to adapt to a new normal; it's perhaps less understood how much the new normal will be shaped by the normalizations of neural networks, how much the clinical triage triggered by the virus is figurative of the long-term algorithmic distribution of life chances.

One early warning sign was the way that AI completely failed to live up to its supposed potential as a predictive tool when it came to COVID-19 itself. More than a year into the pandemic, there was enough evidence for medical researchers to evaluate the performance of machine learning tools in diagnosis and prognosis, that is, in predicting who had caught the virus and who, having caught it, would become seriously ill. The early days of the pandemic were a heady time for AI practitioners as it seemed like a moment where new mechanisms of data-driven insight would show their true mettle. "I thought, 'If there's any time that AI could prove its usefulness, it's now. I had my hopes up'", said one epidemiologist (Heaven, 2021). Overall, the studies showed that none of the many hundreds of tools that had been developed made any real difference, and that some were in fact potentially harmful (Wynants et al, 2020; Driggs et al, 2021). While the authors of the studies attributed the problem to poor datasets and 'disconnects between research standards in the medical and machine learning communities' (Wynants et al, 2020; Driggs et al, 2021), this explanation fails to account for the deeper social dynamics that were made starkly visible by the pandemic response, or the potential for AI to drive and amplify those dynamics.

In the UK, guidelines applied during the first wave of COVID-19 said that patients with autism, mental disorders or learning disabilities should be considered 'frail', meaning that they would not be given priority for treatment such as ventilators. Some local doctors sent out blanket Do Not Resuscitate notices to disabled people. The social shock of the pandemic resurfaced visceral social assumptions about 'fitness', which shaped both policy and individual medical decision-making, and were reflected in the statistics for deaths of disabled people (Office for National Statistics, 2020a). The UK government's policy-making breached its duties to disabled people under both its own Equality Act and under the UN Convention on the Rights of Persons with Disabilities (Tidball, 2020). "It's been extraordinary to see the speed and spread of soft eugenic practices", said an academic from Oxford University. "There are clearly systems being put in place to judge who is and isn't worthy of treatment" (Quarmby, 2020).

At the same time, it became starkly obvious that Black and ethnic minority communities in the UK were hit by a disproportionate number of deaths due to COVID-19 (Office for National Statistics, 2020b). While initial attempts to explain this reached for genetic determinism and the kind of race science tropes we discussed earlier, these kinds of health inequities occur primarily because of underlying histories of structural injustice. Social determinants of health, such as race, poverty and disability, increase the likelihood of pre-existing health conditions, such as chronic lung disease or cardiac issues, which are risk factors for COVID-19; poor housing conditions, such as mould, increase other co-morbidities, such as asthma; and people in precarious work may simply be unable to work from home or even afford to self-isolate. So much sickness is itself a form of structural violence, and these social determinants of health are precisely the pressure points that will be further squeezed by AI's automated extractivism.

By compressing the time axis of mortality and spreading the immediate threat across all social classes, the pandemic made visible the scope of unnecessary deaths deemed acceptable by government. In terms of deaths that can be directly traced to UK government policies, for example, the casualties of the pandemic can be added to the estimated 120,000 excess deaths linked to the first few years of austerity (Watkins et al, 2017). The COVID-19 pandemic has cast a coldly revealing light not only on the tattered state of social provision but also on a state strategy that considers certain demographics to be disposable. The public narrative about the pandemic became underpinned by an unspoken commitment to the survival of the fittest, as the deaths of those with 'underlying health conditions' were portrayed as regrettable but somehow unavoidable. Given the UK government's callous blustering about so-called 'herd immunity', it's unsurprising to read right-wing newspaper commentary claiming that, 'from an entirely disinterested economic perspective, the COVID-19 might even prove mildly beneficial in the long term by disproportionately culling elderly dependents' (Jeremy Warner in *The Telegraph*, cited in Tilley, 2020).

Appalling as this may be in itself, it's important to probe more deeply into the underlying perspective that it draws from. What's at stake is not simply economic optimization but a deeper social calculus. The economization of life, which treats economy and population as mutually articulated objects of governance, is not only linked to gross domestic product (GDP) but to sedimented ideas of population strength as a metric of power. The national strength, in the case of the UK and many other western nations, is bound up with a continuous and unbroken coloniality. A deep-seated fear that underlies the acceptability of 'culling' your own population is that a frail White population is a drain, one that makes the nation vulnerable to decline and replacement by immigrants from its former colonies (Tilley, 2018). AI is a fellow traveller in this journey of ultranationalist population optimization because of its usefulness as a mechanism of segregation, racialization and exclusion. After all, the most fundamental decision boundary is between those who can live and those who must be allowed to die.

Predictive algorithms act as a mechanism of 'state racism' (Foucault, 2003, cited in Spade, 2015), whose operations subdivide resources down to the level of the body, identifying some as worthy and others as threats or drains. AI will thus become the form of governance that post-colonial philosopher Achille Mbembe calls necropolitics: the operation of 'making live/letting die' (Mbembé and Meintjes, 2003, pp 11–40). Necropolitics is state power that not only discriminates in allocating support for life but sanctions the operations that allow death. It is the dynamic of organized neglect, where resources such as housing or healthcare are subject to deliberate scarcification and people are made vulnerable to harms that would otherwise be preventable. Mbembe uses the concept of necropolitics to frame the continuation of relations that were established with slavery, plantations and colonization. The abolitionist Ruth Wilson Gilmore has a definition of racism which neatly sums up its inherent necropolitics: 'Racism, specifically, is the state-sanctioned or extralegal production and exploitation of group-differentiated vulnerability to premature death' (Gilmore, 2006, p 28).

The designation of disposability can be applied not only to race but along any decision boundary. Socially applied AI acts necropolitically by accepting structural conditions as a given and projecting the attribute of being suboptimal onto its subjects, as per the previously cited examples of post-austerity welfare.

Expendability becomes something innate to the individual. The mechanism for enacting this expendability is rooted in the state of exception: AI becomes the connection between mathematical correlation and the idea of the camp as the zone of bare life. In Agamben's philosophy the camp is pivotal because it makes the state of exception a permanent territorial feature. The threat of AI states of exception is the computational production of the virtual camp as an ever-present feature in the flow of algorithmic decision-making. As Mbembe says, the camp's origin is to be found in the project to divide humans: the camp form appears in colonial wars of conquest, in civil wars, under fascist regimes, and now as a sink point for the large-scale movements of refugees and internally displaced people. 'Division and occupation go hand in hand with expulsion and deportation, and often also with an avowed or disavowed program of elimination. When all is said and done, not for nothing will the camp-form have accompanied, practically everywhere, logics of the eliminatory settlement' (Mbembe and Corcoran, 2019, p 127).

Eugenics

There's a long history of entanglement between the logics of elimination and the mathematics that powers AI. Mathematical methods like regression, which came up in Chapter 1 when we looked at the core operations of machine learning, originate in the concept of 'regression to the mean', derived by the aforementioned Francis Galton as part of his efforts to develop a metrics of Social Darwinism. The ideas of Social Darwinism emerged around the same time as, and in dialogue with, Darwin's theory of natural selection, but they were developed by different people and with different ends in mind. One of the leading exponents was British philosopher Herbert Spencer, who saw being poor as a sign of being socially unfit. It was Darwin's *On The Origin of Species* that handed him the language of scientific credibility for his social elitism, and in turn Spencer coined the term 'the survival of the fittest' to describe Darwin's theory. While Spencer was happy to let poverty and neglect kill off the poor, later Social Darwinists felt that active intervention was needed. As prominent eugenicist Madison Grant wrote in his book, *The Passing of the Great Race*: 'the laws of nature require the obliteration of the unfit, and human life is valuable only when it is of use to the community or race' (Grant, 1921, p 167).

Galton, who was Charles Darwin's half-cousin, was convinced that the survival of the fittest applied to human society and that intelligence was the measure of superior fitness. He wanted to assert the heritability of intelligence as an explanatory factor for social and racial hierarchies. Foreshadowing machine learning's predictive methods, Galton wanted to develop a mathematics for social intervention. His goal was to encourage an overall betterment of society through selective breeding, encouraging the production of offspring by high-intelligence parents and discouraging those with lower intelligence from having children. Galton called his programme 'eugenics', meaning 'well-born' (Allen, 2001). He established the first scientific department for the promotion of eugenics at University College London, and was succeeded there by his protégé Karl Pearson.

Pearson developed the concept of the correlation coefficient, which is central to both statistics in general and machine learning in particular. But he also spent time measuring skulls gathered from across the Empire, especially from Africa, and developed a 'coefficient of racial likeness', on the basis that the statistical comparison of skull measurements would unequivocally determine race. Core work in the creation of statistical methods as we now know them was being conducted alongside the pursuit of a racial imperialist view of national progress. In a lecture to members of the Literary and Philosophical Society, Pearson said: 'My view – and I think it may be called the scientific view of a nation – is that of an organized whole, kept up to a high pitch of internal efficiency by insuring that its numbers are substantially recruited from the better stocks, and kept up to a high pitch of external efficiency by contest, chiefly by way of war with inferior races' (Smith, 2019).

Galton and Pearson were followed as founders of modern statistics by Ronald Fisher, who developed important tests of statistical significance and core concepts such as 'maximum likelihood'. Fisher promoted statistical significance testing as a generalizable decision framework that was applicable to all experimentation. He was also a eugenicist, who's famous book

The Genetical Theory of Natural Selection included sections on 'Economic and biological aspects of class distinctions' and 'The decay of ruling classes' (Clayton, 2020). While many in the science and statistical communities would like to argue that scientific achievements can be wholly disentangled from the beliefs of their originators, what we are pursuing here is the way that political positions are emerging around AI which can be traced directly back to the supremacist agenda that statistical methods were originally developed to serve.

The single most weaponized statistical metric used by eugenicists in modern times has been IQ. Ironically, its originator, French psychologist Alfred Binet, developed the IQ test in order to identify school children who needed additional support, and rejected the idea that it represented a fixed and innate attribute of the individual. But the idea of IQ was seized upon by a researcher at Pearson's Eugenics Laboratory called Charles Spearman. He used statistical reduction on clusters of IQ test results to reveal what he believed was an underlying pattern, which he called 'general intelligence' (the g-factor). His conviction was that superior people had innately superior intelligence, and this intelligence would be observable in a consistent pattern of performance across a variety of intellectual tasks. Spearman and his collaborators built a pyramid of assumptions: that IQ reflects a quantifiable factor called intelligence, that this factor is largely innate, and that it both represents and justifies the existence of observable social hierarchies (Smith, 2019).

The idea that 'intelligence' is a single entity that can be abstracted to a single number has been thoroughly critiqued (Gould, 1996). Different IQ tests, and even different analyses of the same tests, produce variable scores, indicating that whatever IQ is measuring, it is a combination of different things. Moreover, its reliability as a proxy for anything genetic is undermined by the way IQ has increased over recent decades (the so-called Flynn effect). Its dependency on sociocultural factors is evidenced by the way '[c]hildren who are the most socially and economically disadvantaged have been shown to lose IQ points over their summer holidays, while the most advantaged ones gain knowledge and skills over the same time period' (Saini, 2019, chapter 9). The only thing we can really be sure about is that IQ measures people's performance on IQ tests. However, as we'll see shortly, the underlying commitment to a hierarchy of intelligence feeds directly into contemporary beliefs about AI.

IQ was operationalized in the interwar years via US law mandating the exclusion and sterilization of the so-called feeble minded. Measures were targeted at 'low IQ' immigrant ethnic groups who threatened to 'dilute the strength of the United States', and were used to justify their denial of entry at New York's Ellis Island (Smith, 2019). While all-out eugenics fell out of favour after the Second World War because of its association with the crimes of the Nazis, IQ as a metric of racial worth resurfaced during the civil rights era. The idea of an innate IQ difference between races became a core objection to racial equality in the civil rights era, and later resurfaced in popular texts like *The Bell Curve* with its proposals for social policy based on purported connections between race and intelligence. This text assumed that intelligence can be reduced to a number that can then be used to rank people in linear order, that intelligence is primarily genetic, and that the long history of slavery and racism had no significant effect on the data from IQ tests. The cluster of racialized concepts circulating around intelligence and IQ never went away, and are common currency across a new generation of social media reactionaries. To its adherents, the idea of the g-factor is not a statistical pattern but a very real force in the world, and one that explains the existence of observed social differences. The relevance for this book is the way similar beliefs persistently re-emerge in the discourse around AI.

The uncanny effectiveness of AI under certain conditions has been enough, in some people's eyes, to reignite hope in the coming of Artificial General Intelligence (AGI). AGI refers to genuine machine reasoning, not AI's narrow imitation of human behaviour on specific tasks. An AGI system would have the same ability to learn as we do, with a level of autonomy to match, and the problem-solving capacities we normally associate with a conscious, thinking being. In other words, it would display a general intelligence as defined by Spearman. While most enthusiasts of deep learning recognize that it's nowhere near AGI as yet, many still choose to believe that it's an irrevocable step in that direction. Leading research lab OpenAI, for example, was founded in anticipation of AGI and its charter says, 'OpenAI's mission is to ensure that artificial general intelligence (AGI) – by which we mean highly autonomous systems that outperform humans at most economically valuable work – benefits all of humanity' (OpenAI, 2018b). AGI is also the ultimate goal of Alphabet subsidiary DeepMind, whose mission statement is 'to solve intelligence and advance scientific discovery for all'.

The general assumption of AGI believers is that mind is the same as intelligence, which is itself understood as logic and rationality. A commitment to AGI and the associated reification of rationalism often comes with social imaginaries that revolve around intellectual elitism and beliefs about innate and biologized superiority. It's at this point that a belief in AGI starts to evoke deeper historical notions about hierarchies of being. If intelligence is something that can be ranked and is taken as a marker of worth, then that is presumably something that also applies to people. The hierarchy of intelligence, which comes automatically with the concept of AGI, merges with the idea that such a hierarchy already exists in humans. This belief is shared by those AI experts who welcome AGI and those who rail against it in apocalyptic terms; the latter simply fear that they will lose their superior status to a machine. On a pragmatic level, the notion of a natural hierarchy of intelligence isn't a problem for engineering and business elites as it provides a rationale for their privilege, but the historical significance of this perspective is the way it has been deployed to legitimize oppressive social and political orders. In particular, it is a racialized and gendered concept that has been widely applied to justify the domination of one group of people over another, especially under colonialism.

The discourse around AGI all too easily merges with the narrative of racial superiority and White supremacy (Golumbia, 2019). Historically, the need for this narrative drove the emergence of modern ideas of both race and intelligence. It was also entangled with machinery and technology: 'For colonial European powers, superior science and technology were not only the means for conquest, but part of its justification, as they demonstrated the superiority of their intellect and culture' (Cave, 2020). Machinery is both a means for domination and the proof of the innate superiority of those deploying it. AI materializes a bootstrapped hierarchy of being whose very justification is the control of the means to further entrench that same hierarchy.

Hanging over AI is the possibility that the ideology of superior intelligence and the practice of machine learning will unite in the pursuit of a machinic eugenics. Contemporary claims that educational achievement is genetically constrained (Lee et al, 2018), for example, could merge seamlessly with the current expansion of learning technologies based on predictive analytics. The net result would be a data-driven educational apartheid. It's notable that when contemporary eugenicists held a clandestine 'London Conference on Intelligence' on the University College campus in 2017, it was attended by someone who the UK government had appointed to its higher education regulatory body (Rawlinson and Adams, 2018). Genetic determinists can be found lurking in the ranks of government advisors in the UK (Cummings, 2014) and policy wonks in the US (Johnson, 2013) arguing for the 'rational reform' of education, and many other areas besides. The problem with this is not only the instrumentalist allocation of life chances but the question of who gets to decide what kinds of life are worth living. As philosopher of race and tech Ruha Benjamin puts it, 'a belief that humans can be designed better than they are' is really 'a belief that more humans can be like those already deemed superior' (Benjamin, 2019, p 117).

Regression, correlation and the notion of general intelligence mark historical entanglements with eugenics that the field of AI has never fully faced up to. The mathematics of disentanglement that AI draws on were driven by the urge to unmingle the superior and the inferior in the human species, and to use prediction and intervention to prevent the latter from propagating. Separation and segregation are the fundamental operations of both AI and eugenics, and the urgent question is how much this legacy will help to shape a post-AI society. There are certainly strong overlaps between the core operational idea of optimization and a eugenicist perspective on populations. On a more practical level, AI's promise of large-scale efficiencies chimes with the way historical eugenicists 'portrayed themselves as efficiency experts, helping to save society millions of dollars by sterilizing defectives so that the state would not have to care for their offspring' (Allen, 2001). It wouldn't be necessary for AI-driven eugenics to be implemented by anything as crude as forced sterilization: it could simply operate as infrastructural filtering at scale. When basic securities such as nutrition and shelter are made precarious and care is deliberately diverted, people easily fall victim to harmful conditions that are otherwise preventable. It's through this kind of 'letting die' that necropolitics enters fully into neural networks.

Fascism

If there's one thing that history teaches us, it's that we need to be very wary of where the systematic application of discriminative ordering can end up. The necropolitical tendencies that we've outlined in AI resonate with the contemporary turn to far-right politics. This form of politics is re-emerging in the tech industry itself, in various governments and institutions, and in the upsurge of populist and fascist political movements. Some of the apparently opportunistic connections between the far right and AI reveal deeper structural ties. For example, one of the co-founders of the fast-growing AI facial recognition startup Clearview AI, which has contracts with US Immigration and Customs Enforcement (ICE) and the US Attorney's Office for the Southern District of New York, turned out to have 'longstanding ties to far-right extremists' (O'Brien, 2020), while another said he was 'building algorithms to ID all the illegal immigrants for the deportation squads'. One of the investors in Clearview was Peter Thiel, co-founder of PayPal and early investor in Facebook. His big data analytics company Palantir has contracts with the Central Intelligence Agency, the Pentagon, the Homeland Security Department, and provides target analysis for ICE raids. It's not that the AI industry is filled with far-right activists, but rather that strands of reactionary opinion appear rhizomatically across the field of AI. As we shall see, following these strands reveals the descending double helix of AI's technopolitics as it connects the ideologies of statistical rationalism to those of fascism.

The first layer of reactionary politics that forms a visible penumbra around the AI industry can be loosely referred to as 'ultrarationalism' because its most identifiable characteristic is a sociopathic commitment to statistical rationality. This isn't a commonsense rational approach to life but a reification of a rather cold intellectual narrowness that is willing to question any assumption, including that of compassion towards fellow beings, if it falls foul of a specific kind of reasoning. One of the trademarks of tech-style rationalism is a frequent reference to Bayesianism. Bayesian statistics, which is widely used in machine learning, is an interpretation of probability that doesn't focus on frequency of occurrence (the basis of classical statistics) but on expectations representing a prior state of knowledge. The relevant thing here is that Bayesian statistics reflects the state of knowledge about a system and is modified by 'updating your priors' (factoring in new or updated knowledge). Ultrarationalists believe Bayesianism provides a superior approach to any problem compared to actual expertise or lived experience (Harper and Graham, nd). Enthusiasts pride themselves on adopting it not only as an approach to designing machine learning algorithms but as a rational and empirical way of tackling everyday life, without being diverted by anything as misleading as emotion or empathy. It's perhaps unsurprising that such an ethos finds a home in a culture of computer science and AI, especially among those who believe we're on the way to artificial general intelligence: 'In AGI, we see a particular overvaluation of "general intelligence" as not merely the mark of human being, but of human value: everything that is worth anything in being human is captured by "rationality or logic"' (Golumbia, 2019).

This kind of ultrarationalism and its entanglements with artificial intelligence were initially articulated on blogs such as LessWrong, whose progenitor was the self-styled theorist of superintelligent AI, Eliezer Yudkowsky, and on blogs like the ultrarationalist touchstone Slate Star Codex. For all their swagger about science and statistics, the ultrarationalists are so rooted in their innate sense of superiority that they rarely do the background research necessary to really understand a field of thought and often seem happy to make things up simply to prove a point. As noted by Elizabeth Sandifer, a researcher and writer who has studied the ultrarationalists in depth, the standpoint of these blogs resonates strongly with the tech sector because both communities see themselves as iconoclastic, fearlessly overturning established knowledge using only the power of their own clever minds. 'It is no surprise that this has caught on among the tech industry. The tech industry loves disruptors and disruptive thought,' she says, 'But ... [t]he contrarian nature of these ideas makes them appealing to people who maybe don't think enough about the consequences' (Metz, 2021).

Ultrarationalists are unreflective to the point of self-parody. They give their efforts self-aggrandizing labels like 'the Intellectual Dark Web'; their blogs are wordy and full of jargon, mainly to obfuscate their core values; and while they claim to espouse absolute free speech, what they actually produce are convoluted expressions of male privilege and White supremacy. They complain that men are oppressed by feminists and that free thought about innate social differences is stymied by a politically correct mob, but what they really seem enraged about is anyone challenging them. The populist version of rationalism legitimizes patriarchal privilege, particularly for young men, and acts as a gateway to far-right political positions (Peterson, 2018). This in itself pollutes the pool from which AI practitioners are drawn, but ultrarationalism is also directly imbricated in the political economy of AI. Peter Thiel was a friend of Yudkowsky and invested money into his research institute (Metz, 2021). He also invested in two followers of Yudkowsy's blog who started an AI firm called DeepMind, subsequently bought by Google, which shot to fame for developing the Go-playing AlphaGo system. OpenAI was founded as a DeepMind competitor with investment from Elon Musk, and both DeepMind and OpenAI hired from the rationalist community (Metz, 2021). While it's difficult to know what proportion of practitioners entertain these kinds of ideas, the main significance of the ultrarationalist community is the way it acts as a bridge between the AI field and more explicitly authoritarian politics like neoreaction.

Neoreaction, or what one of its founding thinkers, Nick Land, calls 'the Dark Enlightenment' (Land, 2012), is an ideology that embraces and amplifies concepts like data–driven eugenics. It draws from strands of thinking that, like the alt-right and new-wave White supremacy, have their wellspring in online forums and discourse. One thing that distinguishes neoreaction from some of the other manifestations of the online far right, like the frothing misogyny of Gamergate (the online harassment of women and feminism in the game industry) or hate-trolling of 8chan (a message board site with links to White supremacism), is its relative coherence as an ideology. And while neoreaction as a movement may have limited reach, the currents it pulls together are significant because of their alignment with the affordances of AI. In fact, neoreaction can be situated as the theoretical wing of AI-driven necropolitics.

Neoreaction has an explicit commitment to innate hierarchies of gender and intelligence of the kind that, as we've seen, are only too easily reinforced by AI. It evinces an enthusiasm for race science, especially the brand of genetic determinism flagged as human biodiversity, and the race realism that legitimates the concept of human sub-species. Neoreaction's geneticism is mostly focused on IQ as the main driver of socioeconomic status, and it has a vision of a 'genetically self-filtering elite' (Haider, 2017). It is explicitly anti-democratic, seeing democracy as a demonstrably and inevitably failed experiment. It draws on wider currents of libertarianism that argue that, due to the inadequate rationalism of the general public, electoral democracy will 'inevitably lead to a suboptimal economic policy' (Matthews, 2016).

Neoreaction's preferred structures are authoritarian or monarchist, typically taking the form of a corporate state with a chief executive officer (CEO) rather than any kind of elected leader. Names that come up when the leadership role is discussed are people like Peter Thiel, who seems to share many of the same political leanings as neoreaction, or Eric Schmidt, the former CEO of Google/Alphabet. In his 2009 essay for libertarian publication *Cato Unbound*, Thiel declared, 'I no longer believe that freedom and democracy are compatible.' The argument from neoreactionary bloggers is that an 'economically and socially effective government legitimizes itself, with no need for elections' (MacDougald, 2015). Neoreaction is the ascendency of capitalist technocracy without the trappings of electoral legitimacy, and with an almost mystical belief in authority and hierarchy.

These techno-authoritarians sneer at democracy as an outdated operating system which they can replace with their own blend of autocracy and algorithms. One of neoreaction's most prolific interpreters, Curtis Yarvin (aka Mencius Moldbug), calls this neocameralism, a reference to his admiration for the political and bureaucratic system of Frederick the Great of Prussia. The future nation doesn't have citizens but shareholders: 'To a neocameralist, a state is a business which owns a country' (Moldbug, 2007). Given that the combined turnover of the four Silicon Valley giants – Alphabet (Google), Apple, Amazon and Meta – is bigger than the entire economy of Germany, this isn't, perhaps, such an impossible vision. In Nick Land's brand of accelerationist neoreaction, the capitalist system is 'locked in constant revolutionary expansion, moving upwards and outwards on a trajectory of technological and scientific intelligence-generation that would, at the limit, make the leap from its human biological hosts' into a superior artificial intelligence (Matthews, 2016).

> Attempts to stop AI's emergence, moreover, will be futile. The imperatives of competition, whether between firms or states, mean that whatever is technologically feasible is likely to be deployed sooner or later, regardless of political intentions or moral concerns. These are less decisions that are made than things which happen due to irresistible structural dynamics, beyond good and evil. (MacDougald, 2015)

Neoreaction takes the structural dynamics that drive AI's harmfulness and elevates them to teleology.

The general justification offered for these beliefs is that existing systems are palpably imperfect and inefficient, and infected with unempirical beliefs in human equality. Technological advances provide the architecture for a move beyond these feeble dependencies to an optimized future. Neoreaction seems to manifest a pure form of the kind of thoughtlessness that already goes with AI, and a lack of emotional engagement carried to the point of pathology. Under the technocratic world order of neoreaction, people are essentially assets or liabilities, and the latter, whether disabled or neurodivergent or racially inferior, most definitely qualify as being disposable. For all its intellectual pretence, neoreaction is a glorification of existing inequalities and a wish for their intensification, based on the idea that some people are more 'fit' than others, that their privilege is built into their DNA and is demonstrated by their wealth and power. This makes for a heady mix with systems like AI, with their inbuilt tendency to emphasize and accentuate existing disparities of class, gender, race and beyond. Existing technocratic systems already embed these discriminations, but both AI and neoreaction accelerate them.

Ultrarationalism and neoreaction are ideologies that keep AI aligned with White supremacy, but they don't exhaust its full potential for amplifying far-right politics. We are at a critical juncture for AI, not only because it can intensify existing social injustices but because of the rising far-right political forces poised to take advantage of it. We need to consider the potential relationship between AI and fascism. Like the other linkages between social forces and AI that we have considered in this book so far, this is not only a question of AI being adopted by fascist political currents but about the resonances between fascistic politics and AI's base operations.

Fascism is more than an authoritarian way of keeping the system going during difficult times. It's a revolutionary ideology that calls for the overthrow of the status quo on both political and cultural fronts. While AI might seem like a pinnacle of intellectual abstraction, being based on complex mathematics and finely tuned systems of large-scale computing, its reductive segregations of the social make it vulnerable to the kind of anti-intellectualism that fuels populist and fascist ideology. What's at stake with AI is not merely bias and unfairness but assimilation into far-right political projects. For fascist ideologues who glorify violence, AI's tendencies towards epistemic, structural and administrative violence are not flaws but features. There's a danger that the disruptive potential of AI will become entangled with the more savage disruptions of a fascistic social vision.

As we discussed in the Introduction, the core fascist goal is the rebirth of a mythic national community out of a state of impurity and decline. The fascist revolution relies on the identification of an internal enemy whose presence pollutes the organic community of the nation, an enemy which may also be lurking at the borders and threatening to overrun the homeland. According to Nazi philosopher Carl Schmitt, 'the specificity of the political' is the 'discrimination between friend and enemy'. In Schmitt's terms, 'Every actual democracy rests on the principle that not only are equals equal but unequals will not be treated equally. Democracy requires, therefore, first homogeneity and second – if the need arises – elimination or eradication of heterogeneity' (Schmitt, 1988, p 9). It's not hard to see how AI's powers of discrimination and its facility for creating states of exception align with this kind of political project, one where the end goal of social exclusion is some form of eugenics.

The immediate danger is not the adoption of AI by a fully fledged fascist regime but the role of AI in the kind of fascization that we discussed in the Introduction. Witness the ways that state agencies in many countries are already rushing to embrace AI for the purposes of controlling 'out groups' such as immigrants and ethnic minorities, while the European Union, self-styled institutional guardian of the modern Enlightenment, is funding AI-driven border regimes while leaving families to drown in the Mediterranean. The fact that AI is being deployed by states that describe themselves as democracies is cold comfort if we remember that the National Socialist state in Germany in the 1930s was also a constitutional democracy in formal terms, albeit one that was hollowed out by states of exception. Given the historical alliances between fascism and big business, we should also ask whether contemporary AI corporations would baulk at putting the levers of mass correlation at the disposal of regimes of rationalized ethnocentrism. In fact, as the history of corporate complicity suggests, they are likely to find themselves aligned with that fraction of the dominant class which, finding its interests threatened by an unresolvable crisis, throws its weight behind a fascist movement as a last line of defence.

Historical fascism has shown itself as being able to embrace the dissonance of employing new technologies to force a return to an imagined ultra-traditionalist past. Thanks to ideologues like Ernst Jünger and his vision of 'technics born from fire and blood' (Herf, 1986, cited in Malm and The Zetkin Collective, 2021), the Nazis developed a 'reactionary modernism' (Herf, 1986) that appropriated high technology while rejecting modern value systems. The operations of German fascism were only possible because of the affordances of advanced technologies and a compliant bureaucracy. The Nazi regime adopted the pre-computational technology of Hollerith punch card machines, furnished by IBM subsidiary Dehomag (Black, 2012), as an important part of their programme of mass social sorting and their identification of demographics for elimination – those whom the Nazis referred to as *Lebensunwertes Leben*, 'life unworthy of life'. While the ideology of fascism usually focuses on a lost golden age rooted in folk tradition, appealing now to those who feel they've lost out to globalization and technocracy, historical fascism was very pragmatic in its adoption of high tech in the service of an alternate modernity (Paxton, 2005).

Fascism responds to real social contradictions by offering a fake revolution and a catharsis through collective psychosis. 'We are not required to believe that fascist movements can only come to power in an exact replay of the scenario of Mussolini and Hitler. All that is required to fit our model is polarization, deadlock, mass mobilization against internal and external enemies, and complicity by existing elites' (Paxton, 2005). We can't rely on images of past fascism to alert us to its re-emergence because fascism won't do us the favour of returning in the same easily recognizable form, especially when it finds new technological vectors. While AI is a genuinely novel approach to computation, what it offers in terms of social application is a reactionary intensification of existing hierarchies. Likewise, fascism offers the image and experience of revolution without fundamentally altering the relations of production or property ownership. AI is technosocial solutionism, while fascism is ultranationalistic solutionism. The social contradictions that are amplified by AI, and so starkly highlighted by the disparities of COVID-19 and climate change, are the social contradictions that fascism will claim to solve.

We must apply a critical vigilance to the political resonances of AI, especially where it claims to offer greater social efficiency through acts of separation and segregation. The essence of fascism is the setting aside of democracy and due process as a failed project, and the substitution of a more efficacious system of targeted exclusion. Fascism is less a coherent ideological proposition than a set of 'mobilising passions' (Paxton, 2005), at the root of which is a passionate polarization, a struggle between the pure and the corrupt, where one's own ethnic community has become the victim of unassimilable minorities. These are sentiments that justify any action without limits, and fascism pursues redemptive violence without ethical or legal restraint. In fascism, a sense of overwhelming crisis combines with a belief in the primacy of the group to drive national integration through the use of exclusionary violence.

Climate crisis

The crisis which looks most likely to bring about the convergence of AI with a fascistic politics is climate change. The promotional narrative around AI often invokes some unsubstantiated yet vital role in directly mitigating the climate crisis, such as the claim by DeepMind's co-founder Demis Hassabis that their AlphaFold software for predicting protein structures may predict proteins that create renewable biofuels (Revell, 2020). According to Hassabis, an exponential improvement in AI is far more likely to save the world from the climate disaster than changes in human behaviour (Heath, 2018). We've already noted, however, some of the contributions of AI to climate change, such as its reckless energy demands, its consumption of water resources, and its promotion as an accelerant for the fossil fuel industry. AI is already a seamless part of a wider system where extraction follows closely on the heels of abstraction, where everything of the world is seen as a utilitarian resource, not as a component of a fragile ecosystem. But beyond this, the climate crisis projects two of the most problematic aspects of AI onto a giant canvas: its solutionism and its facility for fascization. The primary climate threat posed by AI is not the egregious use of energy to train the models but the idea that AI is key to 'solving' climate change.

The hegemonic approach to climate change, as expressed through the resolutions of recent United Nations Climate Change Conferences, is essentially solutionist. While the rhetoric on global warming is that we're all in it together, actual climate actions reinforce the division between privilege and vulnerability. Rather than responding to the need for actual restructuring of the world system that has fuelled the crisis in the first place, the responses are a mixture of market mechanisms such as carbon offsetting and high-tech fixes such as carbon capture. Given everything we've worked through in previous chapters, it's easy to see how neatly AI falls in with this approach, both as a mechanism for optimizing market mechanisms and as a core component of technical fixes. Moreover, climate change will produce new forms of austerity for AI systems to manage. The climate crisis manifests all of the necropolitical tendencies we've discussed in this chapter, from scarcification to states of exception.

One of the darker portents of neoliberalism's inaction in the face of the climate crisis is the alliance between climate denialism and fascist politics. As extensively documented in the book *White Skin, Black Fuel* (Malm and The Zetkin Collective, 2021), there is a long and ignoble alliance between elites committed to fossil fuel extraction and far-right political movements, which is expressed both by funding and by ideological overlap. The seams of this tendency, which can be termed 'fossil fascism', are as deep as the coal reserves themselves – from the colonialist White supremacism that justifies extracting resources from the Global South to burn in the Global North, to the *Volk*-ish 'blood and soil' bonds between ethnonationalists and the mineral resources that lie beneath. This denialism uses the same kind of diversionary tactics that are implicitly enacted by all solutionism; the problem isn't climate change but the presence of too many immigrants or Muslims disrupting our society and replacing our people. The fascization of AI that lies in wait here is clear; as the collision between continuing extractivism and obvious climate consequences causes a political and social crisis, the fossil elite may switch its full backing to a fascist political solution. At that point, all of the resources of the state are available to the far right, including the segregating powers of AI.

The other potential response is ecofascism, where the existence and consequences of climate change are broadly accepted by far-right political movements but the blame for such consequences is shifted onto racialized targets. In this case, the climate crisis is interpreted as proof of the decadent breakdown of the natural order (Moore and Roberts, 2021). Ecofascism typically blames overpopulation in the Global South for both global warming and for the flow of refugees and migrants into western countries. An example of this can be seen in the recent switch of France's far right *Rassemblement National* (formerly the National Front) from climate denialism to a position of blaming 'planetary nomadism' for destroying 'European ecological civilisation' (Malm and The Zetkin Collective, 2021, p 136). The primary tool of this Malthusian extremism is the border: 'It is by returning to the borders that we will save the planet' and 'The best ally of ecology is the border' (Malm and The Zetkin Collective, 2021, p 136). The dividing practices of AI will also find their place within ecofascism's offer to solve the climate crisis once and for all.

As climate disaster is already a reality for many, with around 7 million people displaced due to extreme weather in the first half of 2019 alone (Dobbe and Whittaker, 2019), the immediate application of AI will be to 'manage' the ensuing crises of climate recession and climate refugees. As philosopher Isabelle Stengers notes in her commentary on the climate crisis, 'humanity is rapidly moving into a state of global apartheid, one organised around questions of security and access to resources' (Beuret, 2017). The fascization of AI under climate change, via whatever combination of fossil fascism or ecofascism, will make it an apparatus not of actual solutions but of segregation and apartheid.

This chapter makes the case that not only does AI amplify neoliberal inequalities but it accelerates the various dimensions of necropolitics, that is, the politics of who gets to live and who does not. This acceleration is a product of resonances between external conditions like austerity and the pandemic, the nature of re-emerging far-right movements, and the character of the operations that AI applies at scale. These are developments that should be met with immediate refusal and resistance. Successful opposition will be grounded on principles that are radically different to, but as powerful as, the ideologies of hierarchy and exclusion that dominate our epistemological frameworks. As

AI itself shows so clearly, how we come to know things shapes how we come to act. In the next chapter we will propose an alternative way of knowing that's based on relationality and mutual care, as a basis for developing, in the final chapters, our proposals for an anti-fascist approach to AI.

5

Post-machinic Learning

The first part of this book charted the thoughtless use of AI as social solutionism, and the way this intensifies structural violence. We've also seen how the feedback between the operations of AI and current political conditions helps to tip the neoliberal status quo further towards forms of necropolitics, up to and including fascism.

As a reaction to this, the remainder of this book will ask how we can resist, interrupt and replace AI. Given the entrenched momentum behind systems that produce algorithmic states of exception, this is going to take more than appeals to ethics or tinkering with regulation. The injustice that flows from applied AI rests on separations in our social structures and conceptual frameworks that go all the way down; any transformative challenge to AI needs to be radical in that it needs to 'proceed from the root'. In this chapter, we'll start the process of developing a radical challenge to AI by tackling some of the deep-rooted exclusions in our ways of understanding the world.

AI is an apparatus that helps to configure reality through specific arrangements of power. The perspectives that it reinforces are fundamentally unaccountable, and limit our options for being and becoming. The path to undoing AI's violence and necropolitics starts with standpoints that are situated and relational. In this chapter we aim to transcend algorithmic exclusions through a perspective of care and mutuality, and to develop this as a basis for an alternative political praxis.

Feminist science

We've seen in earlier chapters how AI draws its legitimacy from statistics and science. The question of how to undo AI's necropolitics is also a question of how to take apart its encircling wall of scientific authority. Fortunately, a lot of the hard work has already been done by thinkers who have challenged science itself from feminist and post-colonial perspectives. In particular, we can make use of the approach to science that came out of standpoint theory.

Standpoint theory suggests the possibility of alternative ways of knowing, rooted in the lived experience of people who are marginalized or minoritized. The term 'minoritized' is used to refer to a social group who is not simply composed of fewer people but is actively devalued by the dominant culture in a given context. Standpoint theory is an alternative to the dominant abstractions of thought, in particular those based on a detachment from the devalued activities of care (Hartsock, 1983, cited in Puig de la Bellacasa, 2017). It is, first and foremost, a challenge to the aura of absolute objectivity that places the scientific method above other ways of knowing. Science was originally able to establish itself as an authority by making the scientist themselves into a neutral and objective observer who simply recorded observations as verifiable facts (Shapin and Schaffer, 2011). Over time, the rising voices of those who were socially marginalized by gender, race or colonization questioned the way that this allegedly neutral 'view from nowhere' always acted in the interest of existing social power while at the same time dismissing any unwelcome critique as subjective and irrational. If AI is allowed to pull off the same trick, it will be much harder to tackle its automated harms. A viewpoint like that of AI, which is by its own estimation above, outside of and unlocated, cannot be held properly to account on its own terms (Haraway, 1988).

Standpoint theory is concerned with the ways that the assumptions, discursive frameworks and conceptual schemes generated by dominant groups get hard coded into the ways the rest of us think about the natural world and about social relations. It's not saying that science just makes things up but that any particular form of science is modulated by the social order in which it develops. It challenges the assumption that the internal features of science, its method and its mathematical representation of the world, make it immune to cultural influence. This is exactly the kind of challenge that people are now having to construct in a hurry to contest the world view imposed by AI. According to standpoint theory, prevailing standards for objectivity are too weak to identify culture-wide assumptions that shape the selection of specific scientific questions in the first place (Harding, 1998). A standpoint approach to AI would likewise question the assumptions that AI is built on and the legitimacy of relying on its mathematics and methods as means by which to even ask the right questions.

The standpoint critique of science parallels contemporary debates about algorithmic justice by highlighting the ways individuals and groups at the margins of society are disproportionally impacted or simply left out. The argument they have in common is the need to centre the perspective of the minoritized (Kalluri, 2020). Standpoint theory debunks algorithmic claims to objectivity by questioning whether that kind of objectivity is ever possible or even desirable. If all knowledge is historically and socially situated, then dispensing with the claims to neutrality that hide its social history actually makes it more objective by making it accountable and by removing the pretence of disembodied superiority. A standpoint approach to science argues that 'starting thought from marginalised lives' (Harding, 1998, p 18) actually provides a more rigorous way of maximizing objectivity than any optimization function can ever do.

The feminist and post-colonial challenge to science has shown that there's no single recipe for 'real science', such that its emergence is a matter of purely internal dynamics. To overcome unexamined assumptions and privilege, feminist science calls for the expansion of the scientific methodology to include 'locating the origin of the problematics', 'uncovering the purpose of the inquiry' and 'establishing a relationship between the inquirer and their subject of inquiry' (Roy, 2004). These calls are equally applicable to AI. Instead of the solutionism that flows from accepting a problem as given, we should start by locating its origins; in other words, become cognisant of the structural forces which have prioritized it. Designing any deep learning project should mean going beyond choosing the best neural network architecture to ask about its purpose, in other words, whose ends it will serve. Perhaps most radically for machine learning, a feminist methodology of science establishes a relationship between the researcher and the research subject. As we'll see later, requiring mutuality from AI not only cuts through the 'view from nowhere' but provides the basis for the political organization necessary to interrupt algorithmic violence, in particular through practices like mutual aid.

Current AI overlooks the work of care that underpins the world, and replaces it with datafied models of reality that are disconnected and domineering. Applying the principles of feminist science to AI is a way to counter the kind of epistemic cleansing that scours actual social relations in order to prepare them for abstraction (Puig de la Bellacasa, 2017, p 87). Feminist standpoint theory contests the way the interests of the powerful are sedimented into knowledge structures, whether that's in orthodox science or machine learning. As Sandra Harding, one of the key theorists of this approach, said: 'a standpoint is not the same as a viewpoint or a perspective, for it requires both science and a political struggle' (Harding, 1998, p 150).

Post-normal AI

If we're going to apply standpoint theory to AI we need forms of practice that counter its scientistic narrowness by centring minoritized voices. For this, we can borrow directly from post-normal science. This was proposed in the 1990s by Silvio Funtowicz and Jerry Ravetz as a way of positioning science within the wider matrix of social factors, especially when 'facts are uncertain, values in dispute, stakes high and decisions urgent' (Funtowicz and Ravetz, 1993). They recognized that the orthodox scientific method couldn't provide enough guidance when dealing with phenomena that were both novel and complex, and whose impacts extended in scale, time and severity. Their focus on situations with uncertain facts, disputed values and an urgent need for decision-making maps exactly onto the crisis-driven context of contemporary AI. Crises are situations where, from the perspective of post-normal science, it is not sufficient to rely on the model of reductionist rationality that has for so long held sway.

The post-normal critique of science highlights the limits of statistics, and therefore of the mathematics behind AI. 'All the statistical algebra and all the statistical computations are of value only to the extent that they add to the process of inference. Often they do not aid in making sound inferences; indeed they may work the other way' (Bailar, 1988, cited in Funtowicz and Ravetz, 1993). The kind of variation that statistics is good at taming tends to be a smaller part of social problems like poverty, health and climate change, where 'random variability – the stuff of p-values and confidence limits, is simply swamped by other kinds of uncertainties in assessing the health risks of chemical exposures, or tracking the movement of an environmental contaminant, or predicting the effects of human activities on global temperature or the ozone layer' (Funtowicz and Ravetz, 1993). For similar reasons, the big problems of human togetherness are not tractable to the narrow scientistic methodology of AI.

Rather than relying on the traditional scientific virtues of certainty and neutrality, the key axes of post-normal science become 'uncertainty' and 'values'. Where situations combine high uncertainty and high decision stakes, post-normal science proposes that the usual scientific domination of 'hard facts' over so-called 'soft values' has been inverted, and values are actually the stronger variables. This highlights, by contrast, the socially regressive methodology of AI. Where post-normal science tries to recognize situations where values actually need to lead science, AI tries to take exactly those kinds of situations and represent them back as problems where data analytics can be relied on more than messy subjectivity. What we need, at the very least, is a post-normal AI that reasserts the centrality of social values.

The post-normal framework has a proposal for how to do this: the extended peer community. Whereas peer review by members of the scientific community is key to the legitimacy of science, and has become the gold standard for all forms of academic knowledge, the post-normal situation requires this to be democratized beyond the boundaries of narrow expertise. 'In post-normal science, the manifold uncertainties in both products and processes require that the relative importance of persons becomes enhanced. Hence the establishment of the legitimacy and competence of participants will inevitably involve broader societal and cultural institutions and movements' (Funtowicz and Ravetz, 1993).

The way to accommodate uncertainty is not statistical parameterization but an open dialogue where technical expertise takes its place at the table alongside social concerns. All those affected by an issue form an extended peer community for effective problem-solving. When applied to AI this becomes an enactment of standpoint theory, where the perspectives of those disproportionately affected become central to deciding the way forward. Participants' direct knowledge of prevailing conditions helps determine both what data is reliable and what responses are most important. The implication of AI's optimization is not only that there is an optimal solution but that other possibilities are suboptimal by definition. A post-normal approach opposes this vision of an ideal hierarchy that can be mathematically actualized and reasserts the role of direct democracy in the face of uncertainty. AI is a method that has statistical distancing at its core and institutional interests deciding its direction, so the extended peer community is not only a way of correcting AI but a way of contesting it. The extended peer community is not simply an ethical add-on but a scientific and political necessity.

Challenging AI's ways of knowing means not only establishing a peer community but questioning what kind of knowledge can actually be created. The insight from standpoint theory is that knowledge is always partial, and not acknowledging this partiality means that knowledge is actually 'taking sides'. We've certainly seen that the generation of knowledge by machine learning risks riding roughshod over the suppressed perspectives of the marginalized. As feminist philosopher of science and technology, Donna Haraway, puts it: 'objectivity turns out to be about particular and specific embodiment and definitely not about the false vision promising transcendence of all limits and responsibility' (Haraway, 1988). According to Haraway and others, how we define our ideas about objectivity extend to the notion of what an object is in the first place and to the blurring of boundaries between self, technology and the world.

As she pointed out when talking about the concept of situated knowledge, 'objectivity cannot be about fixed vision when what counts as an object is precisely what world history turns out to be about' (Haraway, 1988).

The uncertainty that scientific and technical knowledge systems are always dealing with is an uncertainty around boundaries: what counts as 'this' and what counts as 'that'. AI itself is fundamentally in the business of drawing boundaries, of deciding what is included and what is excluded. Adopting AI as our prosthetic, as our extended means of knowing the world, brings certain consequences in how the world becomes objectified. AI runs the constant hazard of associating with regressive ideas about what is objective and natural, from the physiognomy of criminal faces to the paradigms of race realism. One common factor in far-right and fascist ways of understanding the world, for example, is the determination to force certain boundaries and differences to be understood as fixed, natural and irrevocable. If we are aiming instead for an alternative based on care and repair, it matters what we ground our knowledge on. We need a different understanding of the world, one based on caring about what fixes our ideas of matter and meaning in the first place. For an alternative vision that starts from relatedness not division, we can draw on the ideas of new materialism.

New materialism

AI takes sides not simply by being a tool used by the powerful but by its inherent reinforcement of rigid dualisms and representations. As we've seen from the use of genetics to explain social inequality as material and therefore inevitable, it matters how we think about matter itself and the boundary between matter and meaning. AI is not simply a kind of computation but an extension of the deep splits in our ways of knowing and acting which naturalize systemic injustice. Instead of AI's epistemological apartheid, we need alternative ways to navigate the emergence of meanings and things and to challenge them where necessary. For this kind of perspective, we can turn to a body of thought known as 'feminist new materialism', which follows on from feminist approaches to science and AI. New materialism's emphasis on the fluidity of being and on immersive relationality supports the project for a radical reworking of AI.

In the same way that feminist science doesn't abandon objectivity but redefines it, a new materialist approach is realist while at the same time questioning essentialist ideas about what is real. Rather than starting from a world of objects, a new materialist world view takes relationships as fundamental: instead of focusing on the fixity of static entities, the focus is shifted to the process of how things become. It's not about attempting to overthrow the stability of our everyday experience by saying it's all relative, but about paying attention to the ways that boundaries are fixed and how they might be arranged otherwise. Rather than having a mechanical model of the world, focusing on the processes of becoming means we can see how things emerge and potentially how they might emerge differently. Instead of seeing AI as an outside apparatus that takes in data about the world and spits out useful representations, we can see it as immersed in the process of shaping what things, including us, actually become.

The feminist philosopher Judith Butler questioned how meanings come to be materalized when she questioned the inscription of gender onto the body. She described the way discursive practices stabilize over time to produce what we think of as pre-given material realities. The key dynamic is performative repetition where, for example, the repeated use of language and gestures produce the effects they are apparently simply expressing. Butler calls this 'the sedimenting effect of regulated iterability' (Butler, 1993, cited in Mackenzie, 2006); those aspects of gender which are repeated again and again according to custom and culture become experienced as immutable realities. AI shares this character of performative iterability in its approach to producing knowledge about the world. Rather than misunderstanding AI as a way of reflecting reality, even as a distorted or cracked mirror, we can reformulate it as a mode of diffracting reality, as a way of producing differences that become sedimented as fixed realities.

We can develop more of a new materialist understanding of AI by borrowing from the theorist Karen Barad. She sought a way of understanding the world that 'shifts the focus from questions of correspondence between descriptions and reality (e.g., do they mirror nature or culture?) to matters of practices/doings/actions' (Barad, 2003). This corresponds to the position taken in this book – that what's important is not whether AI's representations of the world are accurate but how AI acts as an apparatus that directly helps to produce the world. Barad herself draws heavily from physicist Neils Bohr's interpretation of quantum mechanics, and her reasons for doing so are illuminating; as she says about Bohr's work, 'This account refuses the representationalist fixation on "words" and "things" and the problematic of their relationality, advocating instead a causal relationship between specific exclusionary practices embodied as specific material configurations of the world' (Barad, 2003).

The argument of this book is that AI is best understood in the same way: not as a system that measures and represents the world, but as an apparatus that helps to produce aspects of the world through the specific exclusions it sets up. The point isn't that AI is some fundamental theory of the universe, like quantum mechanics, but that the conceptual reorientation that was required to tackle quantum mechanics is also a useful way to think about AI. We also need to shift our perspective on ideas like representation versus reality, and on the role of boundaries and exclusions in stabilizing inherent uncertainty. We need alternatives to the way AI currently 'solves' these questions via authoritative truth claims that amplify structural injustice.

According to Bohr, the way you measure – the specific set-up of the apparatus – materially affects what you find. This is wave-particle duality: set things up one way, the electron is a wave, set things up another way, and it's a particle. Setting up the apparatus one way excludes the other possibility. And so with AI – it's not a way of viewing the world but an intervention that helps to produce the world that it sees. Setting it up one way or another changes what becomes naturalized and what becomes problematized. The different possibilities of how these can be assigned mark distinct political approaches to the world, especially in the case of ideologies built on essentializing discriminations. AI is an apparatus whose configuration of the world through exclusionary boundaries enacts specific political realities.

In Barad's theory, a specific arrangement or apparatus effects a 'cut' that results in the apparent separation between subject and object, matter and meaning, cause and effect. Thinking about AI as an apparatus that makes a similar kind of cut is a way of understanding the deep relationship between technology and politics. In this picture of the process, AI is a performance of a particular reality that marks out what must be accepted and what can be changed. As we will explore further in the next chapter, the priority must be to interrupt AI's rigid reproduction of reality so as to open up new possibilities for transformation.

Another basic insight of quantum mechanics that we can apply to AI is the inseparability of 'objects of observation' and 'agencies of observation'. In other words, you can't separate observer and observed. Instead of the old classical model where an apparatus can measure the world as it is without affecting it, quantum mechanics ties them together: you can't make an observation without affecting what you're observing. 'Even in the most supposedly abstract cases, the known does reflect back to us and on us. Quantum physicists know this, feminists know this, ethnographers know this' (De Jaegher, 2019). Following on from this, the approach to change taken in the next chapter rests on a foundation of symmetry and mutuality.

Applying this altered perspective to AI means we can have a more process-oriented and relational approach to figuring out an alternative. Process-oriented because the world is not about what 'is' but about the processes by which it comes into being, and relational because those processes are arrangements and re-arrangements of relations in a fundamentally connected world. The takeaway from Barad and Bohr is that nothing precedes originary relationships, which come prior to the things which are related. In the next chapter, we'll explore what that might mean for a transformative politics of AI, in terms of the principles of mutual aid and solidarity and how they should shape our apparatuses. The world of experience comes from what Barad, borrowing directly from Judith Butler, calls 'sedimenting out': the way the repetition of specific divisions lays down the more familiar world of 'this' and 'that'. We can understand AI in the same way: as an apparatus whose repetition and recursion sediments out the world that it is supposedly just predicting. It's by interrupting these repetitions that we can reclaim our collective agency.

Post-machinic learning

Applying standpoint theory and new materialism to our technologies of prediction is a way to learn about the composition of different possibilities. The starting point for opening the realm of the possible, beyond statistical prediction, involves methods of critical pedagogy: that is, collective ways of asking questions about problems we have in common and of determining what is to be done about them. Critical pedagogy is a means of generating new knowledge to tackle shared problems (Freire, 2000) and, equally importantly in our case, of unlearning prior ways of knowing that inhibit the possibility of change. Learning and unlearning together in this way, refusing an absolute separation between observer and observed, is to develop a process of 'thinking with care' (Puig de la Bellacasa, 2017, p 59).

Critical pedagogy is not just about learning what is happening but also about what is not happening and should be, so that we can recast our socio-technical apparatuses as regenerative and not simply as mechanisms for rationing scarcity. In the context of learning about AI and its non-solutions, this means developing both a collective analysis and practical systems that can address problems at a community level. Critical pedagogy develops a situated knowledge that is not fixed or essentialist but is made and remade by our ongoing participation. Embedding critical pedagogy in our structures is a means of contesting machine learning by 'learning against the machine'.

The shock to the system delivered by COVID-19 made it clear that problems can be reinvented and solved beyond the boundaries of the previously possible. When there's a pandemic, it becomes suddenly possible to house the homeless, it becomes possible to provide forms of universal basic income, it becomes possible to have roads that are not filled with choking traffic and skies that are not filled with airline flights and their carbon emissions. It becomes thinkable to change the terms of our social relations in ways that were formerly dismissed as utopian fantasies, and it reminds us that political agency comes from reinventing the problem in a way that is no longer dependent, as AI is, on the prior reality that is given to us.

A post-normal pedagogy of AI requires a radically different approach to probability because the statistical conception of probability that drives current AI inhibits the development of structural alternatives. AI is the steam hammer of limited imagination, a solution to problems defined in administrative offices and enforced through predictive boundaries. If our epistemology is derived only from the world as it is currently realized, it misses the horizon of plurality and difference. Exploring the field of the virtual, the possible but not yet realized, must be done experimentally through the overturning of existing apparatuses and the actualization of something authentically different. While the correlations of AI reproduce the oppressive weight of the past, only the associations of collective imagination can call forth other possible worlds.

Instead of being swamped by algorithmic positivism, it's about making a commitment to what philosopher of science Isabelle Stengers calls 'the possible against the probable' (Majaca and Parisi, 2016). The probable lacks only one thing – to exist. Apart from that, it is ready to be deduced. The possible, however, is literally unpredictable, and the methods of reaching it are utterly different. In the next chapter we propose ways of organizing to demand the possible not the probable. These ways of organizing are based on a prefigurative politics, in that they embody 'within ongoing political praxis of a movement ... those forms of social relations, decision-making, culture and human experience that are the ultimate goal' (Boggs, 1977). Against the narrowing iterations of AI, prefigurative politics is an open-ended iteration of social possibilities.

Matters of care

The approach proposed in this chapter is to recompose the question of AI as a 'matter of care' (Puig de la Bellacasa, 2017). Care acts as an epistemological corrective to AI because it directs attention to situated vulnerability and dependency: care is the opposite of algorithmic detachment and abstraction. AI's optimizations are chimeras, produced by and for a world 'in which people do not have to wash their clothes in water full of raw sewage or walk miles to find clean water, fresh fodder or fuelwood. Where people do not have to struggle with heavy shopping bags and small children in pushchairs on and off buses or dash across dangerous roads to get to the school'. The computations of large-scale models operate at millions of floating point operations per second, not 'at the pace of the toddling child or the elderly person with emphysema' (Mellor, 1997, cited in Puig de la Bellacasa, 2017).

We have argued that a key facet of knowing is not only who decides, but how boundaries are produced and what role our apparatuses play in producing them. Care starts from a concern about the boundaries and exclusions at work in a stratified society (Puig de la Bellacasa, 2017, p 29), which are multiplied and amplified by AI. Approaching AI as a matter of care promotes a focus on the way beings become objectified, and replaces flattening reductiveness with a perspective that takes relationality as fundamental. It 'directs attention to neglected things and devalued doings that are accomplished in every context by the most marginalized ... and to logics of domination that are reproduced or intensified in the name of care' (Puig de la Bellacasa, 2017, p 56). Where the AI industry focuses on building models that gain a few percentage points on an industry benchmark for predictive accuracy, a perspective of care asks how the result might amplify neglect. Starting from the principle of care is a counterproject to AI's thoughtlessness and 'view from nowhere'.

The contrast between current AI and matters of care is not only instructive on the levels of values and epistemology, but also directs our attention back to questions of labour and political economy. Care is the invisibilized labour that is an inevitable consequence of our interdependence. It's not only AI that is built on invisible labour and 'ghost work' – all economically productive activity is sustained by someone else doing the cleaning, child-rearing and sustaining of social bonds and shared understandings. The activity of care is gendered, racialized and devalued as something secondary and less important. It's commodified for those who can pay, and colonialized as part of a global pyramid scheme, where immigrant women workers plug the care gap in wealthier countries while their own caring responsibilities are transferred further down the chain (Fraser, 2016). Austerity increased the intensity of care needs while acting as cover for state and corporate disinvestment from welfare, and is amplified by AI's scaling of precarity. The bottom–up perspective of care is a counterpoint to all the hierarchies of knowledge and labour that are reinforced by AI.

The arrival of COVID-19 suddenly made it a lot harder to ignore the centrality of care work because it was inescapably clear how much we rely on frontline carers, both paid and voluntary. With typical hubris, advocates of AI also suggest that it can take on the work of care through its capacity to target help where it's most needed. But systems that rely on more finely targeted interventions within a neoliberal framework operate as sites for the reproduction of social inequalities (Keddell, 2019). The principle of risk prediction makes AI an apparatus that operates on the basis of threat rather than understanding: securitizing is not caring.

Unsettling AI's scientistic authority has led us to conclude that any change that promotes mutual care must be community-led and must start from the margins. It has also revealed that the question of AI is an iteration of a profound social and epistemological dynamic: the setting of boundaries and exclusions that sediment relations of power. The role of AI in society can't be separated from the way we understand the process of becoming, and the ways our apparatuses affect what is included and what is excluded as a result of that process. The observer can't be completely separated from the observed: the knower and the known are co-emergent. Realizing that knowledge of the world is processual and relational means overcoming the division between knowing and caring.

This chapter has distilled a set of principles for a counterproject to contemporary AI. The question for the next chapter is how to turn these principles into forms of action. To effect a restructuring we need structures of our own, ones that manifest mutuality but have the political traction to push back against necropolitical power. Organizing for change means organizing in ways that support mutuality and situated accountability, and as we will see in the next chapter, this means moving forward under the banner of mutual aid and solidarity.

6

People's Councils

In the first part of this book, we explored the ways that the harms being caused by AI result from resonances between its intrinsic character and surrounding social structures. We looked in particular at its role in reinforcing institutional violence and far-right politics. In the previous chapter, we started to develop a counter-politics of AI by grounding our understanding of boundaries and exclusions in feminist and new materialist perspectives. While this set up an ethics of relatedness and care, we now need to turn that ethics into tactics.

AI as we know it is hurtling towards an irrevocable entanglement with various registers of violence. There's little sign of existing institutions being able or willing to intervene, except to intensify this trend. Those of us who are not content to accept an environment of necropolitical neural networks need ways of coming together to challenge and transform AI – ways that enact alternative values and forms of relating. We need to connect our matters of care to a politics of change. In this chapter we draw on the politics of mutual aid and solidarity to articulate an alternative, one that doesn't stop at interrupting AI but aims to generate a different kind of autonomy through workers' and people's councils.

Solidarity

When searching for a social tactic that enacts an ethics of care, we need look no further than mutual aid. Mutual aid is the voluntary and reciprocal activity of caring for one another under conditions that are always already political. It draws from the dynamic impulse that emerges in moments of crises, where friends, neighbours and strangers come to each other's aid without preconditions, but also emerges in the smallest of everyday interactions where people support each other outside of the market system. Mutual aid manifests the ontology of new materialism: we act for each other because we recognize, at some level, that we are not absolutely divided and separate, that we co-constitute each other in some important way. Mutual aid counters social separation both concretely and ontologically; that is, both as a practical tactic and as a proposition that the world is itself constituted by relations of mutual interdependence. The mobilization of mutual aid is a direct counter to algorithmic segregation and carelessness.

Mutual aid constantly re-emerges as a response to the vicissitudes of neoliberal fragmentation, including situations where the exploitation is powered by algorithmic systems. Many drivers in Jakarta, where the regional Uber-like platforms are Gojek and Grab, are organized into hundreds of mutual aid collectives known as *ojol* (Qadri and Raval, 2021). These communities have basecamps where their members can gather between jobs. They organize mutual aid funds so that the collective contributions of members can provide payouts in the case of accidents or deaths, and even began distributing personal protective equipment during the COVID-19 pandemic. Networked by WhatsApp groups and a sense of commonality, the ojol have a city-wide group that organizes an emergency response when members are involved in a road accident, coordinating 'ambulance escorts' that keep the route clear for any ambulance carrying an ojol member. Although these communities aren't organized as official workplace unions, their power is acknowledged by the digital platforms, who send representatives to the basecamps to get feedback on proposed system changes and app updates.

Our systems of social boundaries and exclusions are increasingly structured by algorithms and AI, and there is an urgent need to restructure them. Gustav Landauer, philosopher of social anarchism, recognized the transformative potential of restructured relationality when he wrote, 'The state is a social relationship, a certain way of people relating to one another. It can be destroyed by creating new social relationships, i.e. by people relating to one another differently' (Sakolsky, 2012). In our highly infrastructured societies, the relationships that need restructuring include those within and between our apparatuses. Rather than starting from the statistical assumption of separability, which always comes with a gradient of power, mutual aid embraces entanglement as a form of levelling. Where the algorithmic delivery of care is scarcified, commoditized and individualized, mutual aid is expansive, anti-discriminatory and collectivized.

The COVID-19 pandemic catapulted the idea of mutual aid from the political margins to the centre of social discourse, at least temporarily. What we saw in many different places were networks of mutual aid groups springing up as the response of ordinary people to the plight of their neighbours and communities under conditions of lockdown. These collectives had the simple mission of making sure no one was hungry or harmed by the necessity of social distancing. Mutual aid re-emerges like this over and over again in response to dire need because institutional responses to crises are inadequate at best or harmful at worst, especially for the already marginalized. In mutual aid, knowing and caring are not sharply divided but flow naturally into direct action, into researching and tackling problems rather than appealing to distant authorities or algorithmic abstractions to solve them. Mutual aid transforms thoughtlessness through the practice of collective care and repair.

Where mutual aid is the means to tackle a shared need, solidarity is the basis for the struggle against the systems that create scarcity. Solidarity is an action-oriented commitment to one another based on the recognition of a shared commonality. Whereas the expansion of AI-powered necropolitics is justified by the assumption of inequality and division, and in its more fascistic forms, of the vertical ranking of life itself (Burley, 2017), solidarity is the simple strength of seeing what is common across all our struggles for justice. There are collective choices to be made about the kind of futures we want, not just the ones we're statistically predicted to have, and solidarity is their starting point. The challenges of social togetherness cannot be solved as an optimization problem: choosing solidarity is to stand against precarity and neglect and their algorithmic naturalization. Solidarity is the inversion of the algorithmic state of exception.

AI's exclusions are always at the same time enclosures, whether that's through the restricted allocation of resources or the elitist creation of knowledge. The historical and repeated patterns of enclosure that established racial capitalism in the first place, such as the enclosure of common land that created conditions for capitalist labour relations (Linebaugh, 2014), find their extension in the boundarying actions of AI, which not only reiterates these enclosures but proliferates new forms at a previously unachievable level of granularity. To contest these new enclosures we can invoke the commons, not only in the traditional form of shared natural and cultural resources, but encompassing forms of organizing, relating and acting. Commoning is the action of taking aspects of the world back into common ownership and stewardship, and of organizing through structures of mutual aid and solidarity. Commoning is both a refusal of segregation and an assertion of the common good.

Starting from the standpoint of the commons is a form of thinking and acting together that directly counters AI solutionism. Adjusting the boundaries between the included and excluded does nothing to challenge the fundamental premise on which exclusionary solutions are based. The real antidote to exclusion isn't inclusion, it's commoning. Rather than requiring a unifying system of representation, the common space allows differences to be generative of common action. Transforming situations from ones based on endless classification and division to ones based on solidarity starts with connecting through common spaces such as workers' and people's councils.

Workers' councils

We have already seen the start of self-organized collective action against the actual and potential harms of AI in the shape of the nascent tech worker movement. The election of Donald Trump became a catalyst for self-organization among workers in the US tech industry. As quickly as the top leadership of AI giants like Facebook and Amazon rushed to cozy up to the new administration (Streitfeld, 2016), elements of the AI workforce tried to oppose the more extreme initiatives. The wave of ideologically far-right initiatives spilling out of the Trump administration led to a trajectory of tech worker actions, starting with an open letter against the idea of a 'Muslim registry' (Lind, 2016). At the same time, people were becoming collectively aware of the different ways their own companies exemplified the abuse of power, especially in instances of gender or racial bias, which are 'the modalities through which class is lived' (Hall et al, 2013, p 394). A mass walkout at Google was triggered by egregious cases of sexual harassment and cover-up, but quickly became a protest about racism and the exploitation of precarious workers, as well as about all forms of gender-based discrimination (West et al, 2019). This wave of tech worker agitation led to a campaign inside Google that successfully pressured it to drop Project Maven, the company's involvement in developing AI for drone targeting (Shane et al, 2018).

The locus of tech worker activism expanded to address the use of facial recognition technologies by the police and the deployment of AI-driven data mining by US ICE in order to target immigration raids (Saleh, 2019). By clashing with their bosses during these campaigns, tech workers realized something of their proletarian status (Tarnoff, 2020): rather than having a genuine say in what the technologies they created got used for, their experience was unambiguously that of waged workers in the capitalist system who neither own nor control the means of production. This stirring of tech worker self-organization happened at the same time as a wave of struggles by those precarious workers 'below the algorithm', with protests happening at Amazon warehouses (Dzieza, 2020a) and the growth of militant base-level union organization among the algorithmically governed gig workers in companies like Uber and Deliveroo (Parfitt, 2018). Workers who had been both misrepresented (as self-employed) and manipulated (as precarious platform workers) began discovering their own recomposition as a collective subject. According to a researcher of the tech worker movement, 'one theme that figures prominently in statements and interviews is the demand for greater worker control. Across the movement's many mobilizations, workers have demanded greater control over the conditions of their work, how their workplaces are run and organized, and what kind of work they do' (Tarnoff, 2020).

Workers at the heart of creating high-tech automation, as well as those subjugated to it, are starting to seek more self-direction and autonomy. There's a desire for more democracy in the tech workplace as people realize that their efforts are being used for anti-democratic purposes. The challenge is how to turn these demands into structural change. Real change requires more than the reformist demand to break up the tech industry, which wouldn't address the underlying power relations between companies and tech workers, or between AI systems and their precaritized subjects. To match means and ends, the movement of AI workers needs modes of self-organization that can counter AI's harmfulness across the spectrum. This self-organization needs to have as its end goal a fundamental restructuring of the kind that Landauer called 'structural renewal': the construction of parallel socio-technical structures based on horizontality and autonomy (Landauer, 2010). Workers creating AI, and those controlled by it, need a praxis that is as powerful as, but radically different to, the tyrant-friendly hubris of the tech corporations.

For a historically grounded form of workplace organizing with socially transformative potential, we turn to the workers' council. The workers' council is a bottom-up organizational form that has reappeared over and over again in struggles from the early nineteenth century onwards (Cohen, 2011). The workers' council is anti-bureaucratic and directly democratic – an assembly of members making decisions together about matters of immediate concern. It's based on solidarity and self-activity, and the shared sense of a situation that is badly out of balance. As such, it fits the needs of those who want to reclaim their agency within the workplace by collectively exerting their power as workers.

The workers' council is related to but different from that other mode of organizing workers' power, the trade union. Where a traditional trade union depends on hierarchical structures of representation, and on formal recognition by both the company and the law, the workers' council is the self-organized and unmediated engagement of workers in the direct transformation of their conditions. Workers' councils are not only a space for developing counter-power but a form of self-organization that is, unlike most trade unions, explicitly committed to transforming the system. They have historically acted as spaces of rapid consciousness raising and self-education for the participants, not only about immediate issues but about the structural conditions that brought the situation to a point of social conflict. Workers' councils on AI are the means by which workers can learn how to grapple with the enclosing effects of algorithms while unlearning their dependence on the kinds of structures that legitimate those algorithms in the first place.

Like trade unions, workers' councils have more leverage the more people that are involved in them. However, they scale horizontally by reproducing themselves as a confederation rather than through coagulating as hierarchical structures. Coordination is through systems of delegates rather than representatives, where the delegates are people tasked with conveying the position of each council not with making decisions on the behalf of others. This rhizomatic scaling of worker organization is a democratic counter to the scaling effects of AI itself. It also has the capacity to reinforce the vital collaboration between workers 'above' and 'below' the algorithm, as was seen in Amazon during the pandemic when logistics workers on the ground organized with tech workers in corporate headquarters to push not only for safer conditions but for the prioritization of essential shipments to communities (Vgontzas, 2021). It was the local Amazon workers' own organizing committee in Queens, New York, that, in the early days of the pandemic, forced the temporary closure of the warehouse because of unsafe working conditions: 'DBK1 became the first Amazon warehouse in the United States where a coronavirus case was confirmed and where workers won its temporary closure, realizing a slogan [that the organizing committee] had adopted from the prison abolitionist movement: "We keep us safe"' (Vgontzas, 2021).

The Combined Shop Stewards Committee in Lucas Aerospace was one group of high-tech workers who started down the road of transformative change by challenging both their own precaritization and the wider purpose of their work. Lucas Aerospace was an aeronautics and arms company that had been a major UK employer since the First World War, and in 1976, in the face of planned industrial restructuring, a self-organized group of Lucas workers began arguing for the development of social production as a replacement for military contracts. Although it emerged out of trade union activity, the committee quickly took on the characteristics of a workers' council. The committee was made up of shop floor delegates from different sites in the company, and produced an alternative corporate plan that laid out the production of socially useful products instead of weapons ('The Lucas Plan', 2016). Ideas for new products included heat pumps, solar cells, wind turbines, and hybrid power packs for vehicles, making a connection between their immediate struggles and wider concerns about sustainability. All of the 150 designs were generated by consulting ordinary workers and drawing on their knowledge, skills and experience, and the energy and determination of the popular committee were captured in a documentary made at the time for the Open University (Open University, 1978). While the Lucas Aerospace management rejected the plans with considerable hostility, many of the ideas have since become mainstream themes of sustainable technology.

Workers' councils are not a mechanism for the assimilation of workers' voices into the management of the status quo. They are an irruption of an alternative conception of how to organize and how to produce things, even if only in embryonic form. Unlike the repressions magnified by AI, which flow from the resonances between hegemonic politics and technical methods, workers' councils are the start of a transformation rooted in the same material conditions but heading in exactly the opposite direction. Disputes over the abusive working conditions of colleagues or the egregious application of a technology are the tip of the iceberg of a deeper underlying discontent. The decision to set up workers' councils 'does not in itself provide solutions so much as it poses problems' (Debord, 2005, p 68): in particular, it poses the problem of what is to be done about the structures of the status quo.

In effect, workers' councils operate as one of the initial formations of an alternative sociality founded on wider ideas of care, mutual aid and solidarity. Having said that, no structural change can be brought about in the workplace alone. We have already seen the importance of a broad front between tech worker organization and community-based resistance in the campaigns against necropolitical technologies like facial recognition (Stop LAPD Spying Coalition, 2020). As well as workers' councils, we need forms of self-organization that act across production and social reproduction, that is, across the workplace and the community.

People's councils

This book proposes the organization of broad-based intervention in AI through the mechanism of people's councils, in parallel with the workplace organizing of workers' councils. Like the workers' council, the people's council is self-constituting: it isn't granted authority by any institutional structure but asserts itself by the act of people coming together over matters of shared concern. The idea of a people's council is simply that those who are affected by something form a directly democratic body to decide what to do about it. While there's plenty of talk about 'centring the voices of the marginalised' in AI, there's little idea about how to do this in the face of powerful vested interests: a people's council is about giving this principle some political traction.

As AI disproportionately affects those who are already marginalized, a people's council on AI becomes a practical form of standpoint theory and a way of collectivizing that experience and insight. Like the idea of the workers' council, the idea of bottom-up community assemblies has a long political history, and the practice of people's councils tends to re-emerge at times of social crisis or increased authoritarianism. Adopting the horizontal form of the people's council is to structurally oppose the kind of exclusion and exception that is driven forward by AI, and instead to generate relationality and solidarity. People's councils on AI are a way of organizing that creates a counter-subjectivity to abstract segregation, as a means to unite the spaces of technical concern and collective action.

The aim of a people's council on AI is to create a circuit-breaker, where the complexities of situated knowledge can be counterposed to pre-emptive AI solutionism. A people's council on AI can be seen as a militant version of post-normal science's extended peer community, making a space for previously undervalued knowledge and expertise to be mobilized. A people's council on AI is a deliberative assembly that counters epistemic injustice by working on the basis of consensus, because consensus decision-making is a way of 'presencing', of 'slow[ing] the universalizing process by unsettling existing assumptions, boundaries and patterns of political action' (Mitchell, 2015). The iterative sedimentation of algorithmic power is interrupted by the iterative deliberation of those who've been left out, and by the actions that flow from that deliberation.

It's important to distinguish people's councils from watered-down forms of engagement such as citizens' juries, which are currently deployed to deal with questions ranging from AI to climate change. These are often little more than a consultation tool for policy makers or institutions, giving the appearance of deliberative legitimacy while cloaking decisions that are primarily being made elsewhere. Having a question such as 'how best should we address the problem of bias in public sector algorithms?' set by the sponsoring agency, for example, obscures the possibility of rejecting algorithms altogether. Citizens' juries claim to be representative of the population because participants have been selected by a random process such as sortition, although all this really means is demographic diversity in the process of absorption into an institutional agenda. It's not necessarily the case that the citizen's jury form is inherently compromised, and there are examples of it being subverted to pose an authentic challenge to the status quo (Kuruganti et al, 2008), but its representational nature leaves it wide open to assimilation by structures of power. Participating in a citizen's jury is not a form of self-determination but another way of being constructed as a subject, in this case as an 'active citizen'. People's councils, on the other hand, are not a reconfiguring of representative democracy but an exercise in radically democratic self-governance. People's councils are not representative, because they challenge the validity of representation on both political and epistemological grounds. They are instead transformative, because they are constitutive of different subjectivities.

The democratic confederalism being implemented in Rojava, the Autonomous Administration of North and East Syria, shows that local assemblies and people's councils can be viable alternatives to technocratic bureaucracy by opening up a political space for diverse groups and communities (Knapp et al, 2016). These social structures set aside the idea of a top-down system in favour of bottom-up organization, starting with the open assembly of the local commune. A distinctive quality of the social restructuring in Rojava, which makes it even more relevant to countering AI, is that it is explicitly feminist. The patriarchal oppression of women is seen as core to the repressive system as a whole, and the response is both practical (women's co-leadership at all levels, women's armed protection units) and ideological (the development of 'Jineoloji', or the 'science of women'). The development of real communalism in Rojava is a paradigm for the real potential of self-constituting assemblies, underpinned by a feminist critique, to be a counter power to the systemic interests vested in AI.

Like workers' councils, people's councils scale by democratic confederation with one another. People's councils on AI are movement-building mechanisms for the community constraint of machine learning. They mobilize their capacity to act as a counter power by being part of social movements who share their concerns. A people's council that is contesting the deployment of deep learning to manage housing allocation, for example, would situate itself as part of social movements that struggle against homelessness and in favour of fair housing. People's councils are nodes in networks of solidarity building, and common spaces out of which common action can arise. In terms of concrete tactics, it's for the participants to decide where best to intervene: a people's council doesn't map neatly onto the machine learning workflow but positions itself wherever it can be most effective. The people's council is a nomadic intervention in the space of neural networks and their application.

Luddism

Given the specific character of the challenges raised by AI, being at the same time both political and technological, we can ask if there are historical examples of similar struggles that have tactical lessons for us. For an example of resistance under similar conditions, that is, where the top-down imposition of new machinery of production led to increased precarity at a time of already existing economic crisis, we can look to the historical period that participants referred to as 'the Ludding times'.

The Luddite movement of 1811–16 that spread across Nottinghamshire, Manchester and the West Riding of Yorkshire faced an uncannily similar set of dilemmas to contemporary society. Then, as now, the economy was in the throes of a deep crisis, which at that time was caused by the Napoleonic Wars. Then, as now, the introduction of new machinery threatened to radically alter the social relations of power. The introduction of steam- and water-powered shearing and weaving machines into these communities not only changed production itself but also social reproduction and the broader conditions of life. The artisanship of the weavers was undermined by the machines, and the newly created factories were engines for the exploitation of unskilled labour, including women and children. Then, as now, people looked to legal regulation to protect them, but their petitions failed and their statutory protections were repealed. Meanwhile, food prices spiked and their trade was undermined. Under these conditions, the emergence of Luddism was an attempt at the community constraint of harmful technology.

Although they are best known for their machine breaking, the idea that the Luddites were anti-technology *per se* is historical disinformation. These artisans were skilled machinists and adept with complicated looms and table-sized cropping machines (Jones, 2006, p 23). As recognized trades, they had their own charters and rule books and, in effect, a considerable amount of self-governance, and their ways of life and their communities were protected by both guilds and common custom. It was not only their economic situation but their dignity and agency that the new machinery threatened to devastate. We know something of the Luddites' own perspective from a selection of their letters, which were carefully preserved in government archives, gained through operations of spying and repression. These texts illustrate some of the parallels with contemporary struggles around AI because what the Luddites were resisting was not simply the automation of their work but their own reduction and automatization: 'We are at a loss to know where to fix the stigma (too much blame being due to ourselves for not watching better over the trade) as each striving to manufacture on the lowest terms, makes us little better than mere *engines* to support a jealous competition in the market' (emphasis in original) (Binfield, 2004, p 142).

Although the transition to capitalism was well advanced by the time of the Luddites, there was still an element of a 'moral economy' (Thompson, 1993) that restrained capital accumulation and profit-making. The eighteenth-century food riots that preceded the Luddites had at their heart not the looting of food for free but the concept of 'setting the price' at a fair amount for ordinary folk, leading in several instances to the rioters paying for the food they seized at a price they considered to be just. The Luddites transformed this moral economy into a political struggle capable of taking direct action on behalf of the community (Binfield, 2004).

In Yorkshire, for example, Luddite rhetoric shifted over time from making threats to employers for using shearing frames to threats against the local authorities, who they saw as complicit with the new arrangements of exploitation. Likewise, Luddite tactics evolved over time, not so much to leave behind the idea of machine-breaking but to integrate it into a cycle of negotiation, 'combination' – that is, combining together in societies that were like early unions or workers' councils – and insurrection. The most radical side of Luddism combined direct resistance with an alternative social vision. Influenced by the French Revolution and home-grown republican movements, they not only looked backwards to the settled past but forward to the possibility of a people's republic. The Luddite's stance was summed up in a threatening letter to M. Smith, Shearing Frame Holder at Hill End Yorkshire, signed by Ned Ludd, 'clerk to the General Army of the Redressers', which made clear their commitment to 'put down all Machinery hurtful to Commonality' (Binfield, 2004, p57).

The Luddites' reward for challenging enforced subservience to the interests of the machine owners was the imposition of states of exception. The Combination Acts of 1799 had already made trade unionism illegal, machine breaking was made a capital offence, and Luddism was followed by repressive laws like the Seditious Meetings Act. What really wrecked the Luddite movement was infiltration by government spies, echoed in our time by, for example, Amazon hiring the notorious Pinkerton Detective Agency to spy on its warehouse workers (Gurley, 2020). But despite their defeat we should still ask what we can learn from the Luddites, especially as their fears about the impact of machines and manufactories turned out to be right a hundred times over. We should at least ask what we can learn from the heft of a hammer and from the idea that, to paraphrase a later revolutionary, the urge to destroy is also a creative urge.

Certainly, Luddism is a figure for the militancy that is mostly absent from tech critique, but the lessons we can draw on are not only about hammers but about the strength of the community that wielded them. The Luddite resistance took more troops stationed in the north of England to suppress it than the Duke of Wellington took at the same time into the Iberian Peninsula to fight Napoleon. That strength came from solidarity. The Luddites weren't just self-organized, they were a constituent power, asserting their right to define the governance of their trade and, in the end, of their communities. Luddite organization between different areas was based on delegates from local committees, and the post-Luddite insurrectionists of 1820 had plans to set up self-government in Huddersfield (Brooke and Kipling, 1993). Machine breaking was the wildcat action of its time, and the West Riding of Yorkshire was the Rojava of its day.

As we've seen in this book, AI systems are taking on aspects of what the Luddites would call 'obnoxious machines'. The sledgehammer used by the Luddites to smash shearing frames was known as Enoch's hammer, after the blacksmith's workshop of Enoch and James Taylor in Marsden, West Yorkshire, where they were reputedly made. The irony is that the Taylor brothers were also responsible for building a version of the new cropping machines, each one replacing the labour of ten men. Hence the Luddite saying, 'Enoch made them, and Enoch shall break them', a saying which could equally apply to tech worker activism in our time. Given the array of violence amplified by AI, in epistemic, administrative and structural forms, it would be hard to say that the time for machine breaking ever went away. In general, the task for workers' and people's councils is to forge, through struggle, a new kind of hammer to disrupt the naturalization of AI. Historical Luddism shows us what is positive in the act of refusal. A commitment to resistance means creating space for the construction of the commons.

Anti-fascism

Having looked in some length at the political complicities of AI, and after concluding that the way to counter them is with horizontally organized tactics of refusal, we are now in a position to sum up the overall approach proposed by this book, namely, that our approach to AI must be an anti-fascist one. Calling for an anti-fascist approach to AI is not only a reaction to its potential entanglement with far-right politics but a commitment to changing the underlying conditions. 'Broadly speaking, the goal of antifascism is to build fully nonfascist and emancipatory communities' (Shaw, 2020, p 113).

One constant feature of historical anti-fascist movements is their early recognition of the nature of the threat, and their understanding that liberal institutions, whether public or private, will fail to tackle it in time. What we've seen emerging through AI is the optimization of the populace, with the highest price paid by the segregated and excluded. Algorithmic power is applied to the unwanted to determine their disposability. Such systems should be refused outright, not given oxygen by the idea that they can be reformed. But anti-fascism has always been a larger project than simply halting any tendency towards fascism because it recognizes the roots of fascism in the status quo and the urgent need for an alternative.

In this chapter we've laid out the ways that mutual aid and solidarity underpin a counter-politics of AI, and proposed how the council form can turn this into a concrete practice at work and in the community. The people's council and workers' council are forms of self-organization that are immediately to hand, if we choose to pursue them. They don't require permission or approval, and indeed would only be held back by them. This self-activity, combined with Luddite militancy, is the commitment needed to tackle deep learning's necropolitics. Taken together, these practices constitute an anti-fascist approach to AI that acts directly to disrupt the threat while also defending spaces outside of algorithmic capture. In the final chapter we look at the potential for the spaces opened up by an anti-fascist approach to AI, where the inversion of the state of exception can be a gateway to structural renewal, and where tactics of commoning can constitute a real alternative to 'machinery hurtful to the Commonality' (Binfield, 2004, p 57).

7

Anti-fascist AI

In the previous chapter we presented the principles of mutual aid and solidarity as the basis for resisting AI and its associated necropolitics, and proposed the tactics of workers' and people's councils to put this resistance into practice. This chapter develops the idea of an anti-fascist approach to AI as that which goes beyond an immediate resistance to algorithmic violence and fascistic solutionism. An anti-fascist approach to AI is one that shifts the focus from resisting AI to restructuring the conditions that give rise to AI in the first place.

This book began with the details of AI as it is right now so as to draw out the resonances between the technical operations of deep learning and their political effects. Most of the wider impacts we've described are not limited to deep learning but will apply to similar successor systems. Any AI-like apparatus that gets applied to structural inequality will intensify violence and will lean far too easily towards necropolitics. However clever these systems appear to be at making recommendations based on data, they will always fail on a social level because they will never recommend liberatory social change.

The struggle against the fascization of AI precedes AI itself. It's not that AI first comes into existence and we then have to tackle its dodgy politics from scratch, but rather that AI is already part of the system's ongoing violent response to the autonomous activity of ordinary people. Instead of having to invent a plethora of new remedial measures, we can build on the long history of community solidarity generated by people's resistance to exclusion and enclosure.

The very generalizability of AI and the way it comes to bear on different communities and constituencies creates the potential for this resistance to cut across race, gender, sexuality, disability and other forms of demographic division. If the whole of society becomes subsumed by algorithmically ordered relations and enrolled in machinic optimization, then society as a whole also becomes a site for contesting the imposition of those power relations. AI's generalizability and its intensification of social crisis creates a position from which to question the totality of social relations.

This chapter addresses the question of how to transform algorithmic relations through the lens of an anti-fascist approach to AI, that is, a radical stance on AI that militantly opposes solutions based on automated scapegoating while pushing for structural alternatives. Resisting AI solutionism means keeping open the question of what is technically and socially possible. This chapter asks what constructive ideas and directions we can draw on, and takes up the thread of prefigurative change laid out earlier in the book, in particular, the pursuit of the possible rather than the probable as the motivation for our action in the here and now.

Anti-fascist AI

> Nothing's more important than stopping fascism,
> because fascism will stop us all.
>
> Fred Hampton, Black Panther Party
> (Alk et al, 1971)

An anti-fascist approach to AI is something that can only be fully defined, at any given moment, by those who are putting it into practice. Nevertheless, it will have certain identifiable qualities to qualify as such, certain resonances if you like, that mark it out as the project that this book is calling for. Building on our analysis of AI in the preceding chapters, we can say for certain that an anti-fascist approach must be both decolonial and feminist.

AI is colonial both because of the intellectual framework it inherits and due to its racialized practices of exteriorization and exclusion. An anti-fascist approach to AI is decolonial as much as it rejects any form of 'dividing practice' (Adams, 2021) that continues 'the entrenchment of a world of apartness' (Madlingozi, 2018, cited in Adams, 2021). The organs of an anti-fascist approach to AI, such as workers' and people's councils, need to position themselves as decolonial through their centring of Blackness in its political sense. This is not about privileging an identitarian or ontological idea of race, like that which AI itself propagates, but about acknowledging that racialized classifications are 'a prominent form of taxonomizing that indexes the more central concern of subverting taxonomizing gestures writ large' and the need to learn from racialized situatedness that 'inflects a broader concern about forces of taxonomy and how to subvert them' (Bey, 2020, p 100). Dividing practices such as Islamophobia have such mobilizing power that Poland's far-right government, for example, was able to use it as a driver for electoral success despite there being, proportionately, hardly any actual Muslims in Poland.

An anti-fascist approach to AI is already feminist, at least in the form proposed here, as it is built on feminist critiques of tech and feminist ethics of relationality and care. However, it must be explicitly feminist because of the tendency that AI systems have to enable gender-based violence and promote violently patriarchal systems. Take, for example, the Plataforma Tecnológica de Intervención Social (Technological Platform for Social Intervention) in Argentina. Billed as a 'pioneering [case] of the use of AI data by public, private and third sector organizations' (Aranda and Hagerty, 2021), it is a system to predict teenage pregnancy and school dropouts, and claims an accuracy rate of 98.2 per cent. However, while it was Microsoft who developed the actual machine learning, the local partners turned out to be a non-profit founded by a Jesuit Priest and 'an NGO whose founder ... is a Catholic activist, member of Opus Dei and an outspoken opponent of legalizing abortion and offering sex education in schools'. The dataset was gathered by targeting 'indigenous, immigrant, and poor women for intimate surveillance' while the predictive system 'centres on motherhood and public health while ignoring or erasing issues of contraception, abortion, and sexual violence' (Aranda and Hagerty, 2021). The system itself has been primarily applied to families from the indigenous Wichi community, one of the sectors of society targeted for extreme political violence, including sexual violence, by the former military dictatorship of the 1970s and 80s, while the country as a whole has a long history of racialized eugenics intertwined with Catholic ideas about the ideal family. Overall, the platform 'works to re-entrench power structures, norms, and control over women's sexuality and reproduction' and constitutes an 'attempt to automate and black box very old forms of eugenic and Catholic surveillance and control of women's bodies and lives, in new technological and privatized forms' (Aranda and Hagerty, 2021).

The readiness of AI to be applied to borders at all levels, from national territories to cultural and gender norms, can serve to perpetuate violence against women even when it claims to be doing exactly the opposite. European far-right movements, including those with a strong influence on governments, are currently seeking to popularize themselves as the guardians of women's safety in the face of a supposed threat of sexual violence from migrants, especially Muslim men: 'the moral panic surrounding sexual violence is used in an attempt to transform the far right into a movement "defending" women' (Käyhkö, 2019). As it says on a leaflet from the Feminist Anti-Fascism Assembly 'the far-right say they want to stop sexual violence by closing national borders, attacking minorities and returning to "traditional" gender roles' (Wade, 2018). Under these kinds of political influence, the operations of bordering and exclusion are presented as pro-women. A feminist anti-fascist approach to AI anticipates its assimilation into these agendas, and works to disrupt them.

The most effective way to prevent the development of misogynist machine learning is to centre the struggles of women, like those targeted by the Plataforma Tecnológica de Intervención Social, who are currently the most marginalized. The opportunity for centring feminism in an anti-fascist approach to AI comes through positioning it within feminist social movements, such as the movements around housing, working conditions and sexual violence; around LGBTQI and migrant rights, and prison abolition; and, especially, those women-led movements in Latin America, Africa and other parts of the Global South who have been leading the fightback against dictatorship, apartheid and neoliberalism for decades. It also comes from the explicit construction of any new apparatus on the feminist principles discussed in Chapter 5, so that it becomes an infrastructure for mutual and reciprocal relationality whose practical impacts are most determined by those closest to the immediate experience.

An anti-fascist approach to AI is one that is hyper-vigilant towards the opportunities for AI's differentiations, whether based on race, gender or any other categorization, to play in to far-right social agendas. The ideology that fascist movements are always trying to insinuate into the mainstream is that of naturalized difference, of a vertical rank of inferiority and superiority couched in racialized and gendered terms. But these dynamics are not only present in fascism, they are fundamental to our social infrastructures: 'Fascism reveals what has always been: systemic inequality, [W]hite supremacy, patriarchy, and systems of power that remain invisible while infecting all aspects of our lives. A fascist movement makes the implicit explicit and forces us to choose sides' (Burley, 2017). An anti-fascist approach to AI is one that is prepared to 'no-platform' any sign of fascistic solutionism or its normalization. The no-platform tactic of anti-fascism was first practiced in the 1930s, where protestors would rush at the stage to disrupt fascist events and shut down their capacity to recruit and organize. No-platforming the platforms of AI means challenging any and all manifestations of machinery that embed violent exclusions under the guise of solving social problems.

An anti-fascist approach to AI is a positive refusal, a rejection of certain forms of apparatus and a commitment to radical alternatives. It is an absolute refusal of the reactionary politics that insinuate themselves into 'the momentum of large-scale sociotechnical systems' (Winner, 1988, p 21) and a starting point for doing something concrete to reverse the situation. Whereas unconstrained AI acts as a new means of enclosure, with the potential for those enclosures to become zones of exception and elimination, an anti-fascist approach to AI both resists this encroachment and attempts to invert it. The project of an anti-fascist approach to AI, especially as manifested in workers' and people's councils, is the inversion of states of exception by creating and defending spaces of autonomy.

Structural renewal

Throughout this book we've highlighted the structural nature of the inequalities and injustices that are amplified by AI. If nothing else, the new wave of AI helps to illuminate these aspects of our existing order. The aim of an anti-fascist approach to AI is to create space for structural renewal, that is, for the replacement of elements of the current material and political infrastructure with alternatives based on horizontality, autonomy and relationships of reciprocity. As we've seen, one of the drivers of AI's voracious generalizability is its basis in correlation, and an anti-fascist approach to AI contests these correlations with the voluntary association of collective action. Rather than relations which are established by the authority of an algorithm, the important relations are those entered into voluntarily and autonomously. The structural renewal of our infrastructural apparatus means a shift to cooperative labour, commons-based peer production, and other self-organized circuits of the social sphere.

The task for those committed to overcoming AI as we know it is as intellectually challenging as anything involved in the development of deep learning, but it starts from a completely different ethos and has utterly different ends in mind. Technology is welcome where it supports and extends the commonality, where it acts as part of an apparatus for collective wellbeing. Algorithmic solutionism is contested not only by refusing to implement it but by substituting something that inverts it, and the challenge is to find ways of tackling social need through apparatuses and social relations that are multi-scalar and coordinated through networking and confederation. The activities of workers' and people's councils on AI will become truly transformative when they see their day-to-day activity as helping to create a new society in the shell of the old (Industrial Workers of the World, 1905).

The decision about what makes a machine obnoxious, or not, is inseparable from a wider goal of socially useful production. In the

UK, development of the idea of socially useful production in the 1970s and 1980s was, in part, an extension of the thinking behind the Lucas Plan, which we discussed in Chapter 6. Proponents of socially useful production argued that any computer-controlled machinery should allow reprogramming by the workers, and that there should be democratic control of the design process. The principles underpinning socially useful production were that it should revitalize work through the conversion of the productive apparatus; 'fulfil social needs, products or services which are not exclusive to the rich or any other elite'; 'maintain or promote health [and] welfare'; use technologies 'which are interactive with human skills, which enhance those skills, which can be controlled by the worker'; and 'stress maintenance, re-use, [and] re-conditioning' (Smith, 2014). These ideas of worker-led transformations resonated with, and were enriched in dialogue with, various social movements of the time, especially feminism, the peace movement, the radical science movement and the emerging environmental movement.

In a stance that foreshadowed the people's councils proposed in this book, the idea of socially useful production expanded beyond the factory to become a strategy for integrating community and industrial struggles, bringing community groups and activists into the production process. As one activist put it, the processes of socially useful production 'demonstrate the capacity for quite ordinary people to question the direction in which technology is going, and demonstrate in a practical way some of the alternatives, and the processes by which we develop those alternatives' (Cooley, 1987, cited in Smith, 2014). The movement aimed for the restructuring of social relations via practical reasoning that generated socially beneficial knowledge.

We can add to the principles of socially useful production by drawing from other thinkers who have addressed the same challenges. Langdon Winner, for example, theorist of the politics of technology, proposed that 'technologies should be given a scale and structure of the sort that would be immediately intelligible to nonexperts, be built with a higher degree of flexibility and mutability, and be judged according to the degree of dependency they tend to foster' (Winner, 2002, cited in Gordon, 2009). The work of philosopher and social critic Ivan Illich is also relevant, especially his 1973 text, *Tools for Conviviality*. By tools, Illich was referring to something like our definition of apparatus: definitely the machinic elements, but also their surrounding institutional arrangements. The conviviality he was aiming for was that tools should enable 'autonomous and creative' activity rather than producing conditioned responses or automatization (Illich, [1973] 1975, p 24):

> A convivial society should be designed to allow all its members the most autonomous action by means of tools least controlled by others. People feel joy, as opposed to mere pleasure, to the extent that their activities are creative; while the growth of tools beyond a certain point increases regimentation, dependence, exploitation, and impotence. (Illich, [1973] 1975, p 34)

For Illich, a vital part of producing convivial technology was the idea of negative design criteria to define the limits within which tools are kept. He recognized the necropolitical potential of contemporary apparatuses, and his method for defining these limits, which he called counterfoil research, was intended not only to 'devise tools and tool-systems that optimize the balance of life, thereby maximizing liberty for all' but to detect 'the incipient stages of murderous logic in a tool'. As with the Luddites, Illich felt it was vital to limit the scope of tools in order to enable social justice (McQuillan, 2016). Rather than putting his faith in juridical mechanisms, Illich argued that convivial tools were themselves the basis for more just arrangements by transforming institutional immiseration into a creative and autonomous interrelationship. As much as tools and technologies are the rolling sedimentation of our social relationships, our decisions about technologies like AI should be explicit about our preferred social futures.

Commoning

We said at the start of this chapter that it's not necessary to invent a whole new approach to AI, but that we can draw on existing forms of community solidarity. One example of an active alternative with elements of socially useful production is the so-called solidarity economy. The concept of a solidarity economy aims to 'link self-managed and worker-owned collectives, cooperative financial organisations and socially-responsible consumption practices to create expanding economic networks whose surpluses are invested in social and ecological regeneration' (Carson, 2021). The key features of solidarity economies are democratic self-governance and a commitment to transformative system change: participants aim to go beyond the idea of a social economy within the status quo and to push for structural renewal. The practice of solidarity economies, in the form of socially based cooperation networks, is a major part of contemporary social movements in Latin America. In Brazil, for example, 'favelas come together in *mutirão* collective work sessions for infrastructure upgrades, such as building sewerage systems or cleaning up abandoned lots; and *favelados* (favela residents) have come together in work collectives' (Carson, 2021). The elements that make up these networks 'are conceived not just as individually following principles of social and environmental justice, but providing inputs for each other, to create an inter-cooperative, self-expanding system' (Carson, 2021).

Solidarity economies are a response to several of the forms of crises that we have tagged as potentially fascism-inducing, from austerity to climate change. The grassroots movements that make up these solidarity economies emerged in Latin America under military dictatorship and expanded under the neoliberal austerity measures of the 1990s. These 'popular economies' and 'institutions of the commons' operate in areas where austerity and repression have devastated lives and livelihoods. Solidarity economies put into practice many of the principles we have already proposed for workers' and people's councils on AI. Their occupations, reinventions and recoveries have been led by neighbourhood councils and communitarian assemblies. Whatever form is taken by an anti-fascist approach to AI, it should support these solidarity economies to challenge the algorithmic intensification of precarity and authoritarianism. An anti-fascist approach to

AI is the construction of an apparatus at the service of a solidarity economy.

It may be that the transformation of AI comes, in part, through its occupation. There are many instances where workers have reacted to austerity-driven shutdowns by occupying their workplaces and transforming material production in collaboration with the local community (Pazos, 2018). While the factory occupations that followed the financial collapse in Argentina in 2001, for example, looked, at first sight, like self-organized versions of the traditional workplace, they went beyond this to establish themselves as centres of the neighbourhoods' culture and community. As a result, they came to be seen as part of the shared commons, and 'when past owners [tried] to evict the workers or seize back the machinery, the whole populace typically [turned] out in solidarity with the workers to prevent such action' (Carson, 2021, p 194). Given that AI is not yet fully cemented into our systems of social and material reproduction, one option for an anti-fascist approach is to figure out how to most effectively 'occupy AI'.

The understanding of the commons used both in the previous chapter and here go beyond the 'common pool resources' featured in Elinor Ostrom's seminal work on the topic (Ostrom, 2009), where she focused on traditional commons like water resources, fisheries and forests. In this book, we have expanded the notion of the commons to include both shared material resources and forms of organizing based on mutual aid and horizontal cooperation. The commons is not an abstraction but a call to action that stands against the enclosure of the interdependencies of life itself. The sucking up of the last drops of groundwater by insatiable data centres in the desert, or the predation of private corporations on the genetic data of genome-wide association studies, are merely symptoms of the way 'commons such as water, education, genetic heritage or culture are increasingly privatized in the name of a financial state of exception' (Caperchi, 2012).

What constitutes the material or social commons is not a historical curiosity but a matter of continuous contestation. New areas of the commons come into political existence when access is disrupted by privatization or bureaucratization, and the relationality of the community to the commons needs to be reasserted (Mattei, 2011, cited in Caperchi, 2012). It is perhaps no surprise that the author of the most cited argument against the commons ('The Tragedy of the Commons') also advocated a White supremacist 'lifeboat ethics' that explicitly argued for the maintenance of American privilege and wealth and the exclusion of poor immigrants at all costs (Garrett, 1974). AI as we currently know it is part of the ongoing process of extending exclusionary boundaries and control into those parts of life that still sustain activity outside of markets and hierarchies. Current AI is an engine of un-commoning, while the goal of an anti-fascist approach to AI is the construction of an apparatus for the expansion of the commons.

The activity of commoning is not only defensive, to defend against further enclosures, but expansive, to open spaces of different relationality and alternative material production. Participation in activities like workers' and people's councils on AI is part of recomposing collectivity so as to move beyond algorithmic precarity and necropolitics: 'The commoner is a constituent participant, the subjectivity that is foundational and necessary for constituting a democratic society based on open sharing of the common. The action of "commoning" must be oriented not only toward the access to and self-management of shared wealth but also the construction of forms of political organization' (Hardt and Negri, 2012, p 89). The commons is a counter metapolitics, making sense of social interventions that are seen as insignificant in isolation but which, taken together, constitute constructive system change. For AI to be part of this change, it must replace optimization with commonization. Rather than accepting that AI should serve the state of exception, an anti-fascist approach to AI supports the materialization of the commonwealth.

A new apparatus

Our ambition should stretch beyond the timid idea of AI governance, which accepts what we're already being subjected to, and instead look to transform our apparatuses into a technical practice that supports the common good. Over the last three chapters we have attempted to conceptualize the starting point for a new apparatus as grounded in relational care, propose tactics for resisting existing AI through workers' and people's councils, and (in this chapter) set out some parameters for an anti-fascist approach that combines feminist and decolonial resistance with creating space for alternatives. The closing remarks that now follow will attempt a preliminary description of what a new apparatus might look like.

As discussed in the Introduction, an apparatus like AI is a layered and interdependent arrangement of technology, institutions and ideology, and any alternative apparatus will also encompass these dimensions. When we're talking about a new apparatus, we're interested in concrete technical and organizational arrangements that resonate with alternative visions of the social. It's highly unlikely that this new apparatus will simply be a repurposing of existing AI for progressive social ends. Tempting as it might be to look at the continent-spanning logistics of a corporation like Walmart and imagine it reordered for social benefit (Rozworski and Philips, 2019), or to wish for accelerated automation across healthcare and manufacturing that delivers luxury for society as a whole (Bastani, 2020), everything we've looked at in terms of the coupling of technical and social orders tells us that this won't pan out as we might hope. Existing systems, and AI perhaps most of all, are not simply tools that can be turned to good ends or bad but technosocial infrastructures with an established momentum. A new apparatus will bear as much resemblance to existing AI as the eco-social innovations of the Lucas Plan did to the tanks and planes produced by Lucas Aerospace.

It's not possible to say at this stage whether a new apparatus, the new coupling of means and ends, will involve advanced computation. The trajectory of a sustainable society must surely be towards alternative technologies that are more ecologically aligned. The COP26 United Nations Climate Change Conference that was held during the writing of this book was a vivid demonstration, as if one were needed, that high-tech solutionism driven by finance capital is an explosive mixture that guarantees increased global warming. Even conceiving of the problems of our planet in terms of a metric of carbon parts per million is a solutionist framing, a 'ready-made problem', and erases the required reworking of all social, technical and ecological relations. One thing we can say with some certainty is that our new apparatus is unlikely to be architectured in the form of giant server farms. The exponential scaling of computing power is complicit with the economic ideology of unconstrained growth. Perhaps we already have all the computing that we need, and the future is more about recycling, salvaging and repurposing. A free society is its own performance of unfolding complexity, whether or not elements of that rest on digital computation.

Probably the most important quality of a new apparatus is that, rather than striving for autonomous computation, it acts as a support for social autonomy. AI as we know it is a technology enrolled in eliminating residual instances of people's autonomy, whether that is fractional breaks from labour in an Amazon warehouse or the ability for desperate refugees to move across a border. AI is at the cutting edge of the ongoing effort to subsume all human activity into the sphere of production and consumption, which 'increasingly exploits the entire range of our productive capacities, our bodies and our minds, our capacities for communication, our intelligence and creativity, our affective relations with each other, and more. Life itself has been put to work' (Hardt and Negri, 2012, p 16). As we've seen, the apparatus in which AI is enrolled delivers both precarity and necropolitical authoritarianism. A new apparatus seeks to invert the state of exception by enabling an ongoing exodus from these relations of exploitation. It is characterized by devolved decision-making and doing, in forms of organization for which workers' and people's councils are the experimental prototypes. A new apparatus involves technology not in a reinstrumentation of wage labour as we know it but a transition to work under conditions of autonomy: cooperative, horizontal and non-coercive. It dissolves the separation from the means of doing that is central to our exploitation. Rather than continuing AI's endless fragmentation of productive activity into separated shards of experience, a new apparatus enables transition by supporting the recomposition of collective subjects – the autonomous form of 'us' that doesn't require a 'them' to justify its existence because the 'us'-ness comes from mutually constituting solidarity.

The framing of a new apparatus accepts that the diversity, variety and complexity of experience overflows representation and is therefore immune to abstraction. Rather, the aim is to support a system that devolves responsibility to the people closest to any given context. It will manifest as the infrastructuring of multiple overlapping networks of local and specific sociality and self-organization that, like workers' and people's councils, will be based on local autonomy and horizontal communication. An important feature, one that is already common in many forms of computation, is the element of recursion; the structures of the new apparatus will be nested within each other as levels of reinforcing activity rather than as rigid pyramids of authority. There will be 'higher' levels of coordination but not in the sense of centralizing authority; rather, to resolve and coordinate issues that need to be decided in common. The tendency to return to bureaucratic forms needs to be held in check, for example, by establishing mutual powers of veto between the different layers. The reductive top-down rational ordering of bureaucracy, including in its high-tech manifestation as AI, is a primary vector for the eliminatory logics of the state of exception. In many ways the new apparatus builds on forgotten, or rather repressed, histories – both social, in the genealogy of worker's and people's councils, and technical, as in projects that prioritized social production and experiments with socialized cybernetics (Medina, 2014). Recursion and networked complexity are aspects that tend to be present in adaptive systems, which is why they are important for the new apparatus. Under current conditions of ecological as well as social stress, the one thing we can be sure of is the need for effective adaptation. In this regard, the new apparatus is the inversion of AI, especially the latter's reliance on recapitulating the recent past and its violent brittleness in the face of unexpected change. The new apparatus isn't striving to 'solve' anything but to sustain the delivery of systems of care and social reproduction under changing conditions, in ways that contribute to collective emancipation. An anti-fascist approach to resisting AI is the experimental and practical construction of this new apparatus.

References

Abreu, M. (2014) 'Incalculable Loss', *The New Inquiry*, 19 August. Available at: https://thenewinquiry.com/incalculable-loss/ (Accessed: 11 December 2020).

Adams, R. (2021) 'Can Artificial Intelligence Be Decolonized?', *Interdisciplinary Science Reviews*, 46(1–2), pp 176–97. doi:10.1080/03080188.2020.1840225.

Agamben, G. (2005) *State of Exception*. 1st edition. Translated by K. Attell. Chicago, IL: University of Chicago Press.

Agüera y Arcas, B., Mitchell, M. and Todorov, A. (2017) 'Physiognomy's New Clothes', *Medium*, 7 May. Available at: https://medium.com/@blaisea/physiognomys-new-clothes-f2d4b59fdd6a (Accessed: 20 February 2022).

Airbnb, Inc (2019) 'United States Patent: Determining Trustworthiness and Compatability of a Person'. Available at: https://pdfpiw.uspto.gov/.piw?docid=10169708&PageNum=1&&IDKey=FA62C959569F&HomeUrl=http://patft.uspto.gov/netacgi/nph-Parser?Sect1=PTO2%2526Sect2=HITOFF%2526p=1%2526u=%25252Fnetahtml%25252FPTO%25252Fsearch-bool.html%2526r=3%2526f=G%25261=50%2526co1=AND%2526d=PTXT%2526s1=airbnb%2526s2=trait%2526OS=airbnb%252BAND%252Btrait%2526RS=airbnb%252BAND%252Btrait (Accessed: 11 December 2020).

Alcorn, M.A., Li, Q., Gong, Z., Wang, C., Mai, L., Ku, W-S., et al (2019) 'Strike (with) a Pose: Neural Networks Are Easily Fooled by Strange Poses of Familiar Objects', *arXiv:1811.11553 [cs]* [Preprint]. Available at: http://arxiv.org/abs/1811.11553 (Accessed: 21 December 2020).

Ali, S.M. (2019) '"White Crisis" and/as "Existential Risk," or the Entangled Apocalypticism of Artificial Intelligence', *Zygon*, 54(1), pp 207–24. doi: 10.1111/zygo.12498.

Alk, H. (Director) (1971) *The Murder of Fred Hampton*. Chicago, IL: The Film Group.

Allen, G.E. (2001) 'Is a New Eugenics Afoot?', *Science*, 294(5540), pp 59–61. doi:10.1126/science.1066325.

Allen QC, R. and Masters, D. (2021) 'The Pandemic, Social Benefits, and Automated Decision Making (ADM): Just Because It Is Quicker to Use a Machine, Is It Consistent with the Principle of Non-discrimination?', *AI Law Blog*, 19 April. Available at: https://ai-lawhub.com/2021/04/19/the-pandemic-social-benefits-and-automated-decision-making-adm-just-because-it-is-quicker-to-use-a-machine-is-it-consistent-with-the-principle-of-non-discrimination/ (Accessed: 11 November 2021).

Alston, P. (2018) 'Statement on Visit to the United Kingdom, by Professor Philip Alston, United Nations Special Rapporteur on Extreme Poverty and Human Rights', *The Office of the United Nations High Commissioner for Human Rights* (OHCHR). Available at: https://www.ohchr.org/EN/NewsEvents/Pages/DisplayNews.aspx?NewsID=23881&LangID=E (Accessed: 11 September 2019).

Alston, P. (2019) 'The Digital Welfare State – Report of the Special Rapporteur on Extreme Poverty and Human Rights'. Available at: https://srpovertyorg.files.wordpress.com/2019/10/a_74_48037_advanceuneditedversion-1.pdf (Accessed 1 December 2019).

Angwin, J., Larson, J., Mattu, S. and Kirchner, L. (2016) 'Machine Bias: There's Software Used Across the Country to Predict Future Criminals. And it's Biased Against Blacks', *Propublica*, 23 May. Available at: https://www.propublica.org/article/machine-bias-risk-assessments-in-criminal-sentencing (Accessed: 6 August 2016).

Aranda, F. and Hagerty, A. (2021) 'Algorithmic Expectations: Foresight and Predestination in a Predictive Model for Teenage Pregnancy', in *2021 Summer School on the Histories of AI: A Genealogy of Power*, paper presented at 'Histories of Artificial Intelligence: A Genealogy of Power' Sawyer Seminar at the University of Cambridge, and was held online 12–16 July 2021. Available at: https://www.ai.hps.cam.ac.uk/summer-school (Accessed: 16 July 2021).

Arendt, H. (2006) *Eichmann in Jerusalem: A Report on the Banality of Evil*. 1st edition. New York, NY: Penguin Classics.

Arvidsson, A. (2016) 'Facebook and Finance: On the Social Logic of the Derivative', *Theory, Culture & Society*, 33(6), pp 3–23. doi:10.1177/0263276416658104.

Asbury, K. and Plomin, R. (2013) *G is for Genes: The Impact of Genetics on Education and Achievement: 13*. 1st edition. Chichester, UK: Wiley-Blackwell.

Athalye, A. et al (2018) 'Synthesizing Robust Adversarial Examples', *arXiv:1707.07397 [cs]* [Preprint]. Available at: http://arxiv.org/abs/1707.07397 (Accessed: 21 December 2020).

Babbage, C. (2010) *On the Economy of Machinery and Manufactures*. Cambridge, UK: Cambridge University Press. doi:10.1017/CBO9780511696374.

Barad, K. (2003) 'Posthumanist Performativity: Toward an Understanding of How Matter Comes to Matter', *Signs: Journal of Women in Culture and Society*, 28(3), pp 801–31. doi:10.1086/345321.

Barr B., Taylor-Robinson, D., Stuckler, D., Loopstra, R., Reeves, A. and Whitehead, M. (2016) '"First, Do No Harm": Are Disability Assessments Associated with Adverse Trends in Mental Health? A Longitudinal Ecological Study', *Journal of Epidemiology & Community Health*, 70(4), pp 339–45. doi:10.1136/jech-2015-206209.

Bastani, A. (2020) *Fully Automated Luxury Communism: A Manifesto*. Reprint edition. London; New York: Verso Books.

Bauman, Z. (1989) *Modernity and the Holocaust*. Cambridge; UK: Polity Press.

Belkhir, L. and Elmeligi, A. (2018) 'Assessing ICT Global Emissions Footprint: Trends to 2040 & Recommendations', *Journal of Cleaner Production*, 177, pp 448–63. doi:10.1016/j.jclepro.2017.12.239.

Bengio, Y., Lecun, Y. and Hinton, G. (2021) 'Deep Learning for AI', *Communications of the ACM*, 64(7), pp 58–65. doi:10.1145/3448250.

Benjamin, R. (2019) *Race After Technology: Abolitionist Tools for the New Jim Code*. 1st edition. Medford, MA: Polity.

Benjamin, W. (2002) *Walter Benjamin: 1913-1926 v. 1: Selected Writings. Revised ed. edition.* Edited by M.W. Jenning and M. Bullock. Cambridge, MA: Harvard University Press.

Benjamin, W. (2005) *Theses on the Concept of History.* New York, NY: Verso. Available at: http://www.versobooks.com/books/29-fire-alarm (Accessed: 11 December 2020).

Berardi, F.B. (2011) *After the Future.* Illustrated edition. Edited by G. Genosko and N. Thoburn. Oakland, CA: AK Press.

Beuret, N. (2017) 'Review: Isabelle Stengers, "In Catastrophic Times: Resisting the Coming Barbarism"', *Theory, Culture & Society.* Available at: https://www.theoryculturesociety.org/blog/review-isabelle-stengers-in-catastrophic-times-resisting-the-coming-barbarism (Accessed: 25 December 2020).

Bey, M. (2020) *Anarcho-blackness: Notes Toward a Black Anarchism.* Chico, CA: AK Press.

Bij Voorbaat Verdacht (2020) 'Een kijkje in de black box van SyRI', *Bij Voorbaat Verdacht,* 25 January. Available at: https://bijvoorbaatverdacht.nl/een-kijkje-in-de-black-box-van-syri/ (Accessed: 14 April 2021).

Binfield, K. (ed) (2004) *Writings of the Luddites.* Baltimore, MD: Johns Hopkins University Press.

Birhane, A. and Cummins, F. (2019) 'Algorithmic Injustices: Towards a Relational Ethics', *arXiv:1912.07376* [cs] [Preprint]. Available at: http://arxiv.org/abs/1912.07376 (Accessed: 18 April 2020).

Black, E. (2012) *IBM and the Holocaust: The Strategic Alliance Between Nazi Germany and America's Most Powerful Corporation.* Expanded edition. Washington, DC: Dialog Press.

Blue, V. (2020) 'Your Online Activity Is Now Effectively a Social "Credit Score"', *Engadget,* 17 January. Available at: https://www.engadget.com/2020-01-17-your-online-activity-effectively-social-credit-score-airbnb.html (Accessed: 11 December 2020).

Boggs, C. (1977) 'Marxism, Prefigurative Communism, and the Problem of Workers' Control', *Radical America,* 11. Available at: https://theanarchistlibrary.org/library/carl-boggs-marxism-prefigurative-communism-and-the-problem-of-workers-control (Accessed: 25 December 2020).

Bolukbasi, T., Chang, K-W., Zou, J., Saligrama, V. and Kalai, A. (2016) 'Man is to Computer Programmer as Woman is to Homemaker? Debiasing Word Embeddings', *arXiv:1607.06520* [cs, stat] [Preprint]. Available at: http://arxiv.org/abs/1607.06520 (Accessed: 21 December 2020).

Bornstein, A.M. (2016) 'Is Artificial Intelligence Permanently Inscrutable?', *Nautilus*, 29 August. Available at: http://nautil.us/issue/40/learning/is-artificial-intelligence-permanently-inscrutable (Accessed: 6 December 2020).

Bostrom, N. (2014) *Superintelligence: Paths, Dangers, Strategies.* Illustrated edition. Oxford, UK: OUP Oxford.

Branwen, G. (2011) 'The Neural Net Tank Urban Legend'. Available at: https://www.gwern.net/Tanks (Accessed: 20 February 2022).

Braun, I. (2018) 'High-Risk Citizens', *AlgorithmWatch*, 4 July. Available at: https://algorithmwatch.org/en/high-risk-citizens (Accessed: 8 April 2021).

Brooke, A. and Kipling, L. (1993) *Liberty or Death: Radicals, Republicans and Luddites, 1793–1823.* 1st edition. Honley, UK: Workers' History Publications.

Brugger, P. (2001) 'From Haunted Brain to Haunted Science: A Cognitive Neuroscience View of Paranormal and Pseudoscientific Thought', in J. Houran and R. Lange (eds) *Hauntings and Poltergeists: Multidisciplinary Perspectives.* Jefferson, NC: McFarland, pp 195–213.

Buolamwini, J. and Gebru, T. (2018) 'Gender Shades: Intersectional Accuracy Disparities in Commercial Gender Classification', in *Conference on Fairness, Accountability and Transparency. Conference on Fairness, Accountability and Transparency*, PMLR, pp 77–91. Available at: http://proceedings.mlr.press/v81/buolamwini18a.html (Accessed: 6 December 2020).

Burgess, M. and Kobie, N. (2019) 'The Messy, Cautionary Tale of How Babylon Disrupted the NHS', *Wired UK*, 18 March. Available at: https://www.wired.co.uk/article/babylon-health-nhs (Accessed: 24 July 2021).

Burke, G., Mendoza, M., Linderman, J. and Tarm, M. (2021) 'How ShotSpotter – an AI-Powered Gunshot-Detecting Device – Landed a Chicago Grandfather in Jail for Nearly a Year with Scant Evidence', *Chicago Tribune*, 20 August.

Available at: https://www.chicagotribune.com/news/criminal-justice/ct-shotspotter-chicago-man-jailed-20210820-krlg7y2gt5gwxozolqvvslsni4-story.html (Accessed: 7 November 2021).

Burley, S. (2017) *Fascism Today: What It Is and How to End It.* Chico, CA: AK Press.

Butler, J. (2011) *Bodies That Matter: On the Discursive Limits of Sex.* 1st edition. Abingdon, UK; New York: Routledge.

Caperchi, G. (2012) 'Defining the Commons', *The Genealogy of Consent*, 29 October. Available at: https://thegocblog.com/2012/10/29/defining-the-commons/ (Accessed: 18 August 2021).

Caruana, R., Lou, Y., Gehrke J., Koch, P., Sturm, M. and Elhadad, N. (2015) 'Intelligible Models for HealthCare: Predicting Pneumonia Risk and Hospital 30-day Readmission', in *Proceedings of the 21th ACM SIGKDD International Conference on Knowledge Discovery and Data Mining.* New York, NY, USA: Association for Computing Machinery (KDD '15), pp 1721–30. doi:10.1145/2783258.2788613.

Carson, K.A. (2021) *Exodus: General Idea of the Revolution in the XXI Century.* Independently published.

Castelle, M. (2018) 'Social Theory for Generative Networks (and Vice Versa)', *castelle.org*, 28 September. Available at: https://castelle.org/pages/social-theory-for-generative-networks-and-vice-versa.html (Accessed: 11 December 2020).

Cave, S. (2020) 'The Problem with Intelligence: Its Value-Laden History and the Future of AI', in *Proceedings of the AAAI/ACM Conference on AI, Ethics, and Society.* New York, NY: Association for Computing Machinery (AIES '20), pp 29–35. doi:10.1145/3375627.3375813.

Chander, S. and Jakubowska, E. (2021) 'EU's AI Law Needs Major Changes to Prevent Discrimination and Mass Surveillance', European Digital Rights (EDRi). Available at: https://edri.org/our-work/eus-ai-law-needs-major-changes-to-prevent-discrimination-and-mass-surveillance/ (Accessed: 23 July 2021).

Charrington, S. (2019) 'Rebooting AI: What's Missing, What's Next with Gary Marcus', The TWIML AI Podcast (formerly This Week in Machine Learning & Artificial Intelligence).

Available at: https://twimlai.com/twiml-talk-298-rebooting-ai-whats-missing-whats-next-with-gary-marcus/ (Accessed: 6 December 2020).

Chen, A. (2019) 'Desperate Venezuelans Are Making Money by Training AI for Self-Driving Cars', *MIT Technology Review*, 22 August. Available at: https://www.technologyreview.com/2019/08/22/65375/venezuela-crisis-platform-work-trains-self-driving-car-ai-data/ (Accessed: 8 November 2021).

Chiel, E. (2016) 'Why Are Sex Workers Getting Kicked Off Airbnb and Other Platforms without Explanation?', *Splinter*, 8 March. Available at: https://splinternews.com/why-are-sex-workers-getting-kicked-off-airbnb-and-other-1793860782 (Accessed: 11 December 2020).

Chow-White, P.A. and Green, S. (2013) 'Data Mining Difference in the Age of Big Data: Communication and the Social Shaping of Genome Technologies from 1998 to 2007', *International Journal of Communication*, 7, p 28.

Chun, W.H.K. (2009) 'Introduction: Race and/as Technology; or, How to Do Things to Race', *Camera Obscura: Feminism, Culture, and Media Studies*, 24(1 (70)), pp 7–35. doi:10.1215/02705346-2008-013.

Ciobanu, C. (2020) 'A Third of Poland Declared "LGBT-Free Zone"', *Balkan Insight*, 25 February. Available at: https://balkaninsight.com/2020/02/25/a-third-of-poland-declared-lgbt-free-zone/ (Accessed: 10 November 2021).

Clarke, R. (2018) 'Why Matt Hancock's Promotion of Babylon Worries Doctors', *The BMJ*, 4 December. Available at: https://blogs.bmj.com/bmj/2018/12/04/rachel-clarke-why-matt-hancocks-promotion-of-babylon-worries-doctors/ (Accessed: 24 July 2021).

Clayton, A. (2020) 'How Eugenics Shaped Statistics', *Nautilus*, 28 October. Available at: http://nautil.us/issue/92/frontiers/how-eugenics-shaped-statistics (Accessed: 24 October 2021).

Coalition for Critical Technology (2020) 'Abolish the #TechToPrisonPipeline', *Medium*, 23 June. Available at: https://medium.com/@CoalitionForCriticalTechnology/abolish-the-techtoprisonpipeline-9b5b14366b16 (Accessed: 15 December 2020).

Cohen, S. (2011) 'Workers' Councils: The Red Mole of Revolution', *The Commune*. Available at: http://libcom.org/library/workers-councils-red-mole-revolution (Accessed: 21 December 2020).

Coleman, R. (2008) 'A Method of Intuition: Becoming, Relationality, Ethics', *History of the Human Sciences*, 21(4), pp 104–23. doi:10.1177/0952695108095514.

Comfort, N. (2018) 'Nature Still Battles Nurture in the Haunting World of Social Genomics', *Nature*, 553(7688), pp 278–80. doi:10.1038/d41586-018-00578-5.

Coop, G. (2018) 'Polygenic Scores and Tea Drinking', *gcbias*, 14 March. Available at: https://gcbias.org/2018/03/14/polygenic-scores-and-tea-drinking/ (Accessed: 9 December 2020).

CRASSH Cambridge (2015) 'Professor Stuart Russell – The Long-Term Future of (Artificial) Intelligence'. Available at: https://www.youtube.com/watch?v=GYQrNfSmQ0M (Accessed: 29 August 2021).

Cummings, D. (2014) ' "Standin" by the Window, Where the Light Is Strong': De-extinction, Machine Intelligence, the Search for Extra-Solar Life, Autonomous Drone Swarms Bombing Parliament, Genetics & IQ, Science & Politics, and Much More @ SciFoo 2014', *Dominic Cummings's Blog*, 19 August. Available at: https://dominiccummings.com/2014/08/19/standin-by-the-window-where-the-light-is-strong-de-extinction-machine-intelligence-the-search-for-extra-solar-life-neural-networks-autonomous-drone-swarms-bombing-parliament-genetics-amp/ (Accessed: 18 December 2020).

Davidow, B. (2014) 'Redlining for the 21st Century', *The Atlantic*, 5 March. Available at: http://www.theatlantic.com/business/archive/2014/03/redlining-for-the-21st-century/284235/ (Accessed: 2 May 2014).

Davies, T., Isakjee, A. and Dhesi, S. (2017) 'Violent Inaction: The Necropolitical Experience of Refugees in Europe', *Antipode*, 49(5), pp 1263–84. doi: 10.1111/anti.12325.

Davis, S. (2019) 'Activists Warn Poland's LGBT Community Is "Under Attack"', *euronews*, 20 August. Available at: https://www.euronews.com/2019/08/20/activists-warn-poland-s-lgbt-community-is-under-attack-the-cube (Accessed: 11 November 2021).

De Jaegher, H. (2019) 'Loving and Knowing: Reflections for an Engaged Epistemology', *Phenomenology and the Cognitive Sciences* [Preprint]. doi:10.1007/s11097-019-09634-5.

Debord, G. (2005) *Society of the Spectacle by Guy Debord*. Oakland, CA: AK Press.

Delaleu, N. (2019) 'Parliament Strongly Condemns "'LGBTI-free zones'" in Poland', *European Parliament News*, 18 December. Available at: https://www.europarl.europa.eu/news/en/press-room/20191212IPR68923/parliament-strongly-condemns-lgbti-free-zones-in-poland (Accessed: 10 November 2021).

Denton, E., Hanna, A. and Amironesei, R. (2021) 'On the Genealogy of Machine Learning Datasets: A Critical History of ImageNet', *Big Data & Society*, 8(2). doi:10.1177/20539517211035955.

Desrosières, A. (2010) *The Politics of Large Numbers: A History of Statistical Reasoning*. Revised edition. Translated by C. Naish. Cambridge, MA: Harvard University Press.

Dickson, B. (2021) 'Pioneers of Deep Learning Think Its Future Is Gonna Be Lit', *TNW*, 5 July. Available at: https://thenextweb.com/news/pioneers-deep-learning-future-lit-syndication (Accessed: 14 July 2021).

Dobbe, R. and Whittaker, M. (2019) 'AI and Climate Change: How They're Connected, and What We Can Do About It', *AI Now*, 17 October. Available at: https://medium.com/@AINowInstitute/ai-and-climate-change-how-theyre-connected-and-what-we-can-do-about-it-6aa8d0f5b32c (Accessed: 16 August 2021).

Dotan, R. and Milli, S. (2020) 'Value-Laden Disciplinary Shifts in Machine Learning', in *Proceedings of the 2020 Conference on Fairness, Accountability, and Transparency*. New York: Association for Computing Machinery (FAT★ '20), p 294. doi:10.1145/3351095.3373157.

Driggs, D., Selby, I., Roberts, M., Gkrania-Klotsas, E., Rudd, J., Yang, G., et al (2021) 'Machine Learning for COVID-19 Diagnosis and Prognostication: Lessons for Amplifying the Signal While Reducing the Noise', *Radiology: Artificial Intelligence*, 3(4), p e210011. doi:10.1148/ryai.2021210011.

Dryer, T. (2021) 'Will Artificial Intelligence Foster or Hamper the Green New Deal?', *AI Now*, 22 April. Available at:

https://medium.com/@AINowInstitute/a-digital-and-green-transition-series-will-artificial-intelligence-foster-or-hamper-the-green-new-bccbe8f779ec (Accessed: 16 August 2021).

Dudbridge, F. (2013) 'Power and Predictive Accuracy of Polygenic Risk Scores', *PLOS Genetics*, 9(3), p e1003348. doi:10.1371/journal.pgen.1003348.

Dzieza, J. (2020a) 'Amazon Warehouse Workers Walk Out in Rising Tide of COVID-19 Protests', *The Verge*, 30 March. Available at: https://www.theverge.com/2020/3/30/21199942/amazon-warehouse-coronavirus-covid-new-york-protest-walkout (Accessed: 24 January 2021).

Dzieza, J. (2020b) 'How Hard Will the Robots Make Us Work?', *The Verge*, 27 February Available at: https://www.theverge.com/2020/2/27/21155254/automation-robots-unemployment-jobs-vs-human-google-amazon (Accessed: 14 April 2021).

Dzodan, F. (2018) 'Machine Learned Cruelty and Border Control', *Artifice of Intelligence*, 19 June. Available at: https://artificeofintelligence.org/machine-learned-cruelty-and-border-control/ (Accessed: 11 December 2020).

Easton, S. (2017) 'Centrelink's Debt Recovery System: Automation Without Good Public Administration', *The Mandarin*, 10 April. Available at: https://www.themandarin.com.au/77738-centrelink-debt-recovery-automation-failed-to-maintain-good-public-administration/ (Accessed: 7 December 2020).

Easton, S. (2019) '"No Apologies" for Robodebt, No Admission of "Mistakes" Despite Major Retroactive Change', *The Mandarin*, 19 November. Available at: https://www.themandarin.com.au/120774-no-apologies-for-robodebt-no-admission-of-mistakes-despite-major-retroactive-change/ (Accessed: 7 December 2020).

Elish, M.C. (2019) 'Moral Crumple Zones: Cautionary Tales in Human–Robot Interaction', *Engaging Science, Technology, and Society*, 5, pp 40–60. doi:10.17351/ests2019.260.

Evans, W. (2019) 'Ruthless Quotas at Amazon Are Maiming Employees', *The Atlantic*, 25 November. Available at: https://www.theatlantic.com/technology/archive/2019/11/amazon-warehouse-reports-show-worker-injuries/602530/ (Accessed: 20 February 2022).

Evelyn, K. (2020) 'Amazon Fires New York Worker Who Led Strike Over Coronavirus Concerns', *The Guardian*, 31 March. Available at: https://www.theguardian.com/us-news/2020/mar/31/amazon-strike-worker-fired-organizing-walkout-chris-smallls (Accessed: 27 December 2020).

Fisher, M. (2009) *Capitalist Realism: Is There No Alternative?* 1st edition. Winchester, UK: Zer0 Books.

Fraser, H. and Wong, D. (2018) 'Safety of Patient-Facing Digital Symptom Checkers', *The Lancet* [Preprint]. doi:10.1016/S0140-6736(18)32819-8.

Fraser, N. (2016) 'Contradictions of Capital and Care', *New Left Review* [Preprint]. Available at: https://www.newleftreview.org/issues/ii100/articles/nancy-fraser-contradictions-of-capital-and-care (Accessed: 7 December 2020).

Freire, P. (2000) *Pedagogy of the Oppressed*. New York; NY: Continuum International Publishing Group.

Fricker, M. (2007) *Epistemic Injustice: Power and the Ethics of Knowing*. Oxford, UK; New York, NY: Oxford University Press.

Funtowicz, S.O. and Ravetz, J.R. (1993) 'Science for the Post-Normal Age', *Futures*, 25(7), pp 739–55. doi:10.1016/0016-3287(93)90022-L.

Galtung, J. (1969) 'Violence, Peace, and Peace Research', *Journal of Peace Research*, 6(3), pp 167–91. doi:10.1177/002234336900600301.

Garrett, H. (1974) 'Lifeboat Ethics: The Case Against Helping the Poor', *Psychology Today*, 10, pp 38–43.

Geng, D. and Veerapaneni, R. (2019) 'Tricking Neural Networks: Create Your Own Adversarial Examples', *Medium*, 7 March. Available at: https://medium.com/@ml.at.berkeley/tricking-neural-networks-create-your-own-adversarial-examples-a61eb7620fd8 (Accessed: 6 January 2021).

Gilmore, R.W. (2006) *Golden Gulag: Prisons, Surplus, Crisis, and Opposition in Globalizing California: 21*. Berkeley, CA: University of California Press.

Go, J. (2021) 'Three Tensions in the Theory of Racial Capitalism', *Sociological Theory*, 39(1), pp 38–47. doi:10.1177/0735275120979822.

Golumbia, D. (2019) 'The Great White Robot God', *Medium*, 1 February. Available at: https://davidgolumbia.medium.com/the-great-white-robot-god-bea8e23943da (Accessed: 6 December 2020).

Gordon, U. (2009) 'Anarchism and the Politics of Technology', *WorkingUSA: The Journal of Labor and Society*, 12(3), pp 489–503. doi:10.1111/j.1743-4580.2009.00250.x.

Gould, S.J. (1996) *The Mismeasure of Man*. Revised and Expanded edition. New York, NY: W.W. Norton & Company.

Grant, C. (2019) 'Data of Prejudice: The Uses and Abuses of the Science of Race', *New Statesman*, 24 July. Available at: https://www.newstatesman.com/Angela-Saini-Jennifer-Eberhardt-race-science-Superior-biased (Accessed: 11 December 2020, link no longer active).

Grant, M. (1921) *The Passing of the Great Race*. 4th edition. New York, NY: C. Scribner's sons, p 167. Available at: http://www.archive.org/stream/passingofgreatra00granuoft/passingofgreatra00granuoft_djvu.txt (Accessed 21 April 2021).

Green, B. (2020) 'Data Science as Political Action: Grounding Data Science in a Politics of Justice', *arXiv:1811.03435 [cs]* [Preprint]. Available at: http://arxiv.org/abs/1811.03435 (Accessed: 6 December 2020).

Griffin, R. (1993) *The Nature of Fascism*. 1st edition. London; New York: Routledge.

Gurley, L.K. (2020) 'Secret Amazon Reports Expose Company Spying on Labor, Environmental Groups', *Vice*, 23 November. Available at: https://www.vice.com/en/article/5dp3yn/amazon-leaked-reports-expose-spying-warehouse-workers-labor-union-environmental-groups-social-movements (Accessed: 30 June 2021).

Gurley, L.K. (2021) 'Amazon's AI Cameras Are Punishing Drivers for Mistakes They Didn't Make', *Motherboard (Vice Magazine)*, 20 September. Available at: https://www.vice.com/en/article/88npjv/amazons-ai-cameras-are-punishing-drivers-for-mistakes-they-didnt-make (Accessed: 18 October 2021).

Haider, S. (2017) 'The Darkness at the End of the Tunnel: Artificial Intelligence and Neoreaction', *Viewpoint Magazine*, 28 March. Available at: https://www.viewpointmag.com/2017/03/28/the-darkness-at-the-end-of-the-tunnel-artificial-intelligence-and-neoreaction/ (Accessed: 23 December 2019).

Hall, S., Critcher, C., Jefferson, T., Clarke, J. and Roberts, B. (2013) *Policing the Crisis: Mugging, the State and Law and Order*. London; UK: Macmillan International Higher Education.

Hanna, A., Denton, E., Smart, A. and Smith-Loud, J. (2020) 'Towards a Critical Race Methodology in Algorithmic Fairness', in *Proceedings of the 2020 Conference on Fairness, Accountability, and Transparency*. New York: Association for Computing Machinery (FAT★ '20), pp 501–12. doi:10.1145/3351095.3372826.

Haraway, D. (1988) 'Situated Knowledges: The Science Question in Feminism and the Privilege of Partial Perspective', *Feminist Studies*, 14(3), pp 575–99. doi:10.2307/3178066.

Haraway, D.J. (1997) *Modest_Witness@Second_Millennium. FemaleMan_Meets_OncoMouse: Feminism and Technoscience*. 1st edition. New York, NY and London, UK: Routledge.

Harding, S. (1998) *Is Science Multicultural?: Postcolonialisms, Feminisms, and Epistemologies*. 1st edition. Bloomington, IN: Indiana University Press.

Hardt, M. and Negri, A. (2012) *Declaración*. New York, NY: Argo Navis

Harper, D. and Graham, J. (nd) 'I Don't Speak German: 82: Scott Alexander & Slate Star Codex, with David Gerard and Elizabeth Sandifer'. Available at: https://idontspeakgerman.lib syn.com/82-scott-alexander-slate-star-codex-with-david-ger ard-and-elizabeth-sandifer (Accessed: 3 August 2021).

Heath, N. (2018) 'Google DeepMind founder Demis Hassabis: Three Truths About AI', *TechRepublic*, 24 September. Available at: https://www.techrepublic.com/article/google-deepmind-founder-demis-hassabis-three-truths-about-ai/ (Accessed: 17 August 2021).

Heaven, W.D. (2021) 'Hundreds of AI Tools Have Been Built to Catch Covid. None of Them Helped', *MIT Technology Review*. Available at: https://www.technologyreview.com/2021/07/30/1030329/machine-learning-ai-failed-covid-hospi tal-diagnosis-pandemic/ (Accessed: 17 October 2021).

Heidegger, M. and Lovitt, W. (1977) *Question Concerning Technology and Other Essays*. Later printing edition. Translated by W. Lovitt. New York, NY: Harper Perennial.

Herf, J. (1986) *Reactionary Modernism: Technology, Culture, and Politics in Weimar and the Third Reich.* Cambridge, UK: Cambridge University Press.

Hsu, J. (2019) 'Medical Advice From a Bot: The Unproven Promise of Babylon Health', *Undark Magazine*, 9 December. Available at: https://undark.org/2019/12/09/babylon-hea lth-artificial-intelligence-medical-advice/ (Accessed: 14 April 2021).

Illich, I. ([1973]1975) *Tools for Conviviality.* Glasgow, UK: Fontana.

Industrial Workers of the World (1905) 'Preamble to the IWW Constitution'. Available at: http://www.iww.org/culture/offic ial/preamble.shtml (Accessed: 9 June 2013).

Ingram, M. (2020) 'Google Silences and then Fires a Black Srtificial-Intelligence Expert', *Columbia Journalism Review*, 10 December. Available at: https://www.cjr.org/the_media_to day/google-researcher.php (Accessed: 25 December 2020).

Jacobsen, J.-H., Geirhos, R. and Michaelis, C. (2020) 'Shortcuts: How Neural Networks Love to Cheat', *The Gradient*, 25 July. Available at: https://thegradient.pub/shortc uts-neural-networks-love-to-cheat/ (Accessed: 21 July 2021).

Jamil, R. (2020) 'Uber and the Making of an Algopticon – Insights From the Daily Life of Montreal Drivers', *Capital & Class*, 44(2), pp 241–60. doi:10.1177/0309816820904031.

Johnson, L. (2013) 'Jason Richwine Resigns From Heritage Foundation After Dissertation Controversy', *HuffPost UK*, 10 May. Available at: https://www.huffpost.com/entry/ jason-richwine-resigns-heritage-foundation_n_3254927 (Accessed: 18 December 2020).

Jones, P. (2020) 'The Deaths of Gig Workers Are Not Freak Incidents, but the Result of a Brutal Business Model', *Novara Media*, 14 January. Available at: https://novaramedia.com/ 2020/01/14/the-deaths-of-gig-workers-are-not-freak-incide nts-but-the-result-of-a-brutal-business-model/ (Accessed: 28 December 2021).

Jones, S.E. (2006) *Against Technology: From the Luddites to Neo-Luddism.* 1st edition. New York, NY: Routledge.

Kafka, F. (2010) *The Trial.* Hollywood, FL: Simon & Brown.

Kalluri, P. (2020) 'Don't Ask if Artificial Intelligence is Good or Fair, Ask How It Shifts Power', *Nature*, 583(7815), pp 169. doi:10.1038/d41586-020-02003-2.

Kantor, J., Weise, K. and Ashford, G. (2021) 'The Amazon That Customers Don't See', *The New York Times*, 15 June. Available at: https://www.nytimes.com/interactive/2021/06/15/us/amazon-workers.html (Accessed: 17 July 2021).

Katz, Y. (2020) *Artificial Whiteness: Politics and Ideology in Artificial Intelligence*. New York, NY: Columbia University Press.

Käyhkö, L. (2019) 'The Feminist Anti-Fascist Assembly: Feminist Movements Are Our Best Chance of Defeating the Far Right', *HOPE not hate,* 8 March. Available at: https://www.hopenothate.org.uk/2019/03/08/feminist-movements-best-chance-defeating-far-right/ (Accessed: 4 September 2021).

Kayser-Bril, N. (2019) 'Spain: Legal Fight Over an Algorithm's Code', *AlgorithmWatch*, 12 August. Available at: https://algorithmwatch.org/en/story/spain-legal-fight-over-an-algorithms-code/ (Accessed: 7 December 2020).

Keddell, E. (2019) 'Algorithmic Justice in Child Protection: Statistical Fairness, Social Justice and the Implications for Practice', *Social Sciences*, 8(10). doi:10.3390/socsci8100281.

Kelley, R.D.G. (2017) 'What Did Cedric Robinson Mean by Racial Capitalism?', *Boston Review*, 12 January. Available at: http://bostonreview.net/race/robin-d-g-kelley-what-did-cedric-robinson-mean-racial-capitalism (Accessed: 1 January 2021).

Khatib, S. (2011) 'Towards a Politics of "Pure Means": Walter Benjamin and the Question of Violence', *Anthropological Materialism*, 28 August. Available at: https://anthropologicalmaterialism.hypotheses.org/1040 (Accessed: 14 December 2020).

Klein, N. (2008) *The Shock Doctrine: The Rise of Disaster Capitalism*. 1st edition. London, UK: Penguin.

Knapp, M., Flach, A. and Ayboga, E. (2016) *Revolution in Rojava: Democratic Autonomy and Women's Liberation in Syrian Kurdistan*. 1st edition. Translated by J. Biehl. London, UK: Pluto Press.

Konkel, F.R. (2016) 'The CIA's Classified Cloud Is Reducing Tasks from Months to Minutes', *Defense One*, 15 December. Available at: https://www.defenseone.com/technology/2016/12/cias-classified-cloud-reducing-tasks-months-minutes/133925/ (Accessed: 7 January 2021).

Krizhevsky, A., Sutskever, I. and Hinton, G.E. (2012) 'ImageNet Classification with Deep Convolutional Neural Networks', *Advances in Neural Information Processing Systems*, 25, pp 1097–105. doi:10.5555/2999134.2999257.

Kuhn, T.S. (1996) *The Structure of Scientific Revolutions*. 3rd edition. Chicago, IL: University of Chicago Press.

Kuruganti, K., Pimbert, M. and Wakeford, T. (2008) 'The People's Vision: UK and Indian Reflections on Prajateerpu', *Participatory Learning and Action*, 58, pp 11–17. International Institute for Environment and Development. Available at: https://pubs.iied.org/g02529 (Accessed: 28 July 2021).

Land, N. (2012) 'The Dark Enlightenment', 2 March. Available at: https://www.thedarkenlightenment.com/the-dark-enlightenment-by-nick-land/ (Accessed: 18 December 2020).

Landauer, G. (2010) *Revolution and Other Writings: A Political Reader*. Edited by G. Kuhn. Oakland, CA: PM Press.

Larson, J., Mattu, S., Kirchner, L. and Angwin, J. (2016) 'How We Analyzed the COMPAS Recidivism Algorithm', *ProPublica*, 23 May. Available at: https://www.propublica.org/article/how-we-analyzed-the-compas-recidivism-algorithm (Accessed: 16 July 2016).

Laurence, J. (2021) '85 Percent of ShotSpotter Alerts are Dead Ends – But Officers Coached to Think They're Responding to Dangerous Situations, Study Finds', *Block Club Chicago*, 5 May. Available at: https://blockclubchicago.org/2021/05/05/85-percent-of-shotspotter-alerts-are-dead-ends-but-they-coach-officers-to-think-theyre-responding-to-dangerous-situations-study-finds/ (Accessed: 7 November 2021).

Lee, D. (2018) 'Why Big Tech Pays Poor Kenyans to Teach Self-Driving Cars', *BBC News*, 3 November. Available at: https://www.bbc.com/news/technology-46055595 (Accessed: 8 November 2021).

Lee, J.J., Wedow, R., Okbay, A., Kong, E., Maghzian, O., Zacher, M., et al (2018) 'Gene Discovery and Polygenic Prediction From a Genome-Wide Association Study of Educational Attainment in 1.1 million Individuals', *Nature Genetics*, 50(8), pp 1112–21. doi:10.1038/s41588-018-0147-3.

Lentin, A. (2018) 'The Future Is Here – Revealing Algorithmic Racism', Alana lentin.net, 22 October. Available at: http://www.alanalentin.net/2018/10/22/the-future-is-here-revealing-algorithmic-racism/ (Accessed: 17 April 2020).

Leon, H. (2020) 'Whole Foods Secretly Upgrades Tech to Target and Squash Unionizing Efforts', *Observer*, 24 April. Available at: https://observer.com/2020/04/amazon-whole-foods-anti-union-technology-heat-map/ (Accessed: 6 December 2020).

Lewell-Buck, E. (2017) 'This Government Is Systematically Failing the Youngest and Most Vulnerable Members of Our Society', *HuffPost UK*, 4 July. Available at: https://www.huffingtonpost.co.uk/emma-lewellbuck/child-poverty_b_17382056.html (Accessed: 11 January 2021).

Lind, D. (2016) 'Donald Trump's Proposed "Muslim registry," Explained', *Vox*, 16 November. Available at: https://www.vox.com/policy-and-politics/2016/11/16/13649764/trump-muslim-register-database (Accessed: 21 December 2020).

Linebaugh, P. (2014) *Stop, Thief!: The Commons, Enclosures, And Resistance*. Oakland, CA: PM Press.

Litsa, E.E., Das, P. and Kavraki, L.E. (2020) 'Prediction of Drug Metabolites Using Neural Machine Translation', *Chemical Science*, 11(47), pp 12777–88. doi:10.1039/D0SC02639E.

MacDougald, P. (2015) 'The Darkness Before the Right', *The Awl*, 28 September. Available at: https://www.theawl.com/2015/09/the-darkness-before-the-right/ (Accessed: 18 April 2020).

Mackenzie, A. (2006) *Transductions: Bodies and Machines at Speed*. New edition. London, UK; New York, NY: Continuum.

Mackenzie, D. (2008) *An Engine, Not a Camera: How Financial Models Shape Markets*. 1st edition. Cambridge, MA: The MIT Press.

Majaca, A. and Parisi, L. (2016) 'The Incomputable and Instrumental Possibility', *e-flux*, (77). Available at: https://www.e-flux.com/journal/77/76322/the-incomputable-and-instrumental-possibility/ (Accessed: 25 December 2020).

Malm, A. and The Zetkin Collective (2021) *White Skin, Black Fuel: On the Danger of Fossil Fascism*. London, UK; New York, NY: Verso.

Massumi, B. (2016) 'Brian Massumi (social thinker)', *TACIT FUTURES Berliner Gazette Annual Conference*. Available at: https://projekte.berlinergazette.de/tacit-futures/ (Accessed: 6 December 2020).

Matthews, D. (2016) 'The Alt-Right Is More Than Warmed-Over White Supremacy. It's That, but Way Way Weirder', *Vox*, 18 April. Available at: https://www.vox.com/2016/4/18/11434098/alt-right-explained (Accessed: 18 December 2020).

Mbembe, A. and Corcoran, S. (2019) *Necropolitics*. Durham, NC: Duke University Press.

Mbembé, J.-A. and Meintjes, L. (2003) 'Necropolitics', *Public Culture*, 15(1), pp 11–40. doi:10.1215/08992363-15-1-11.

McKendrick, D. and Finch, J. (2020) 'Pressure Drop: Securitising and De-Securitising Safeguarding', *Aotearoa New Zealand Social Work*, 32(1), pp 61–72. doi:10.11157/anzswj-vol32iss1id706.

McQuillan, D. (2016) 'Algorithmic Paranoia and the Convivial Alternative', *Big Data & Society*, 3(2). doi:10.1177/2053951716671340.

Medien, K. (2020) 'E103: Internal border controls & NHS charges. (Surviving Society)'. Available at: https://soundcloud.com/user-622675754/e103-kathryn-medien-internal-border-controls-nhs-charges (Accessed: 11 December 2020).

Medina, E. (2014) *Cybernetic Revolutionaries: Technology and Politics in Allende's Chile*. Reprint edition. Cambridge, MA: MIT Press.

Metz, C. (2021) 'Silicon Valley's Safe Space', *The New York Times*, 13 February. Available at: https://www.nytimes.com/2021/02/13/technology/slate-star-codex-rationalists.html (Accessed: 24 April 2021).

Metzinger, T. (2019) 'Ethics Washing Made in Europe', *Der Tagesspiegel*, 8 April. Available at: https://www.tagesspiegel.de/politik/eu-guidelines-ethics-washing-made-in-europe/24195496.html (Accessed: 23 July 2021).

Mitchell, A. (2015) 'Posthumanist Post-Colonialism?', *Worldly*, 26 February. Available at: https://worldlyir.wordpress.com/2015/02/26/posthumanist-postcolonialism/ (Accessed: 17 April 2020).

Moldbug, M. (2007) 'Against Political Freedom', *Unqualified Reservations*, 16 August. Available at: https://www.unqualified-reservations.org/2007/08/against-political-freedom/ (Accessed: 23 January 2021).

Moore, S. and Roberts, A. (2021) 'The Threat of Ecofascism', *The Ecologist*, 25 June. Available at: https://theecologist.org/2021/jun/25/threat-ecofascism (Accessed: 18 August 2021).

Nielsen, M.A. (2019) 'A Visual Proof That Neural Nets Can Compute Any Function', in *Neural Networks and Deep Learning*. Determination Press. Available at: http://neuralnetworksanddeeplearning.com (Accessed: 14 July 2021).

Noack, R. (2019) 'Polish towns advocate "LGBT-free" zones while the ruling party cheers them on', *Washington Post*, 21 July. Available at: https://www.washingtonpost.com/world/europe/polands-right-wing-ruling-party-has-found-a-new-targetlgbt-ideology/2019/07/19/775f25c6-a4ad-11e9-a767-d7ab84aef3e9_story.html (Accessed: 10 November 2021).

Obermeyer, Z., Powers, B., Vogeli, C. and Mullainathan, S. (2019) 'Dissecting Racial Bias in an Algorithm Used to Manage the Health of Populations', *Science*, 366(6464), pp 447–53. doi:10.1126/science.aax2342.

O'Brien, L. (2020) 'Far-Right Extremists Helped Create The World's Most Powerful Facial Recognition Technology', *HuffPost UK*, 9 April. Available at: https://www.huffpost.com/entry/clearview-ai-facial-recognition-alt-right_n_5e7d028bc5b6cb08a92a5c48 (Accessed: 25 April 2021).

Office for National Statistics (2020a) 'Coronavirus (COVID-19) Related Deaths by Disability Status, England and Wales: 2 March to 15 May 2020'. Available at: https://www.ons.gov.uk/peoplepopulationandcommunity/birthsdeathsandmarriages/deaths/articles/coronaviruscovid19relateddeathsbydisabilitystatusenglandandwales/2marchto15may2020 (Accessed: 23 January 2021).

Office for National Statistics (2020b) 'Updating Ethnic Contrasts in Deaths Involving the Coronavirus (COVID-19), England and Wales: Deaths Occurring 2 March to 28 July 2020'. Available at: https://www.ons.gov.uk/peoplepopulationa ndcommunity/birthsdeathsandmarriages/deaths/articles/ updatingethniccontrastsindeathsinvolvingthecoronaviruscov id19englandandwales/deathsoccurring2marchto28july2020 (Accessed: 23 January 2021).

OpenAI (2017) 'Attacking Machine Learning with Adversarial Examples', *OpenAI*, 24 February. Available at: https://ope nai.com/blog/adversarial-example-research/ (Accessed: 6 January 2021).

OpenAI (2018a) 'AI and Compute', *OpenAI*, 16 May. Available at: https://openai.com/blog/ai-and-compute/ (Accessed: 22 December 2020).

OpenAI (2018b) 'OpenAI Charter', *OpenAI*. Available at: https://openai.com/charter/ (Accessed: 6 December 2020).

Open University (1978) 'Lucas Plan Documentary'. Available at: https://www.youtube.com/watch?v=0pgQqfpub-c (Accessed: 22 January 2017).

Ostrom, E. (2009) 'Beyond Markets and States: Polycentric Governance of Complex Economic Systems'. Available at: http:// www.nobelprize.org/nobel_prizes/economic-sciences/laureates/ 2009/ostrom-lecture.html (Accessed: 16 May 2014).

Palheta, U. (2021) 'Fascism, Fascisation, Antifascism', *Historical Materialism* [Preprint]. Available at: https://www.historicalmate rialism.org/blog/fascism-fascisation-antifascism (Accessed: 15 August 2021).

Parfitt, S. (2018) 'Two Tiny but Mighty New Trade Unions Offer UK a Better Way to "Take Back Control"', *The Conversation*, 11 July. Available at: http://theconversation.com/ two-tiny-but-mighty-new-trade-unions-offer-uk-a-better- way-to-take-back-control-99617 (Accessed: 24 January 2021).

Paxton, R.O. (2005) *The Anatomy of Fascism*. London, UK: Penguin.

Pazos, A. (2018) 'Ours to Master and to Own – We Visit Viome, Greece's Only Worker-Managed Factory', *Jacobin*, 10 June. Available at: https://jacobinmag.com/2018/10/viome-self-man agement-factory-takeover-greece (Accessed: 18 April 2020).

Peterson, J.B. (2018) *12 Rules for Life: An Antidote to Chaos.* Reprint edition. London, UK: Allen Lane.

Puig de la Bellacasa, M. (2017) *Matters of Care.* 3rd edition. Minneapolis, MN: University of Minnesota Press.

Qadri, R. and Raval, N. (2021) 'Mutual Aid Stations', *Logic Magazine*, 17 May. Available at: https://logicmag.io/distribut ion/mutual-aid-stations/ (Accessed: 7 November 2021).

Quarmby, K. (2020) 'Under Pressure: Disabled People Mobilise to Defend Their Human Rights', *Liberty Investigates.* Available at: https://libertyinvestigates.org.uk/articles/under-pressure-disabled-people-mobilise-to-defend-their-human-rights/ (Accessed: 15 December 2020).

Rawlinson, K. and Adams, R. (2018) 'UCL to Investigate Eugenics Conference Secretly Held on Campus', *The Guardian*, 11 January. Available at: http://www.theguardian.com/educat ion/2018/jan/10/ucl-to-investigate-secret-eugenics-confere nce-held-on-campus (Accessed: 17 June 2021).

Redman, J. and Fletcher, D.R. (2021) 'Violent Bureaucracy: A Critical Analysis of the British Public Employment Service', *Critical Social Policy*, 42(2), pp 306–26. doi:10.1177/ 02610183211001766.

Reiss, J. and Sprenger, J. (2020) 'Scientific Objectivity', in E.N. Zalta, (ed) *The Stanford Encyclopedia of Philosophy.* Winter 2020 edition. Metaphysics Research Lab, Stanford University. Available at: https://plato.stanford.edu/archi ves/win2020/entries/scientific-objectivity/ (Accessed: 6 December 2020).

Revanche, J. (2018) 'After the "Robo-Debt" Debacle, Traumatised Users Find Support in Online Communities', *The Guardian*, 4 January. Available at: https://www.theguard ian.com/commentisfree/2018/jan/04/after-the-robo-debt-debacle-traumatised-users-find-support-in-online-comm unities (Accessed: 7 December 2020).

Revell, T. (2020) 'Demis Hassabis Interview: Our AI Will Unlock Secrets of How Life Works', *New Scientist*, 30 December. Available at: https://www.newscientist.com/ article/mg24833140-700-demis-hassabis-interview-our-ai-will-unlock-secrets-of-how-life-works/ (Accessed: 17 August 2021).

Richardson, H. (2018) 'Child Poverty: Pale and Hungry Pupils "Fill Pockets With School Food"', *BBC News,* 2 April. Available at: https://www.bbc.com/news/education-43611 527 (Accessed: 16 October 2021).

Robinson, C.J. (2000) *Black Marxism: The Making of the Black Radical Tradition.* New edition. Chapel Hill, NC: University of North Carolina Press.

Roy, D. (2004) 'Feminist Theory in Science: Working Toward a Practical Transformation', *Hypatia,* 19(1), pp 255–79. doi:10.1111/j.1527-2001.2004.tb01277.

Rozworski, M. and Philips, L. (2019) *People's Republic of Walmart: How the World's Biggest Corporations are Laying the Foundation for Socialism.* London, UK; New York, NY: Verso.

Russell, S. (2020) *Human Compatible: Artificial Intelligence and the Problem of Control.* London, UK: Allen Lane.

Saini, A. (2019) *Superior: The Return of Race Science.* 1st edition. Boston, MA: Beacon Press.

Sakolsky, R. (2012) 'Mutual Acquiescence or Mutual Aid?', *The Anarchist Library.* Available at: https://theanarchistlibrary. org/library/ron-sakolsky-mutual-acquiescence-or-mutual-aid (Accessed: 25 December 2020).

Saleh, M. (2019) 'As Trump Announces Mass Immigration Raid, Documents Show How ICE Uses Arrest Quotas', *The Intercept,* 3 July. Available at: https://theintercept.com/2019/ 07/03/ice-raids-arrest-quotas/ (Accessed: 24 January 2021).

Samudzi, Z. (2019) 'Bots Are Terrible at Recognizing Black Faces. Let's Keep it That Way', *The Daily Beast,* 9 February. Available at: https://www.thedailybeast.com/bots-are-terrible-at-recognizing-black-faces-lets-keep-it-that-way (Accessed: 6 December 2020).

Schaffer, S. (1994) 'Babbage's Intelligence: Calculating Engines and the Factory System', *Critical Inquiry,* 21(1), pp 203–27. doi:10.1086/448746.

Schiff, J. (2013) 'The Varieties of Thoughtlessness and the Limits of Thinking', *European Journal of Political Theory,* 12(2), pp 99–115. doi:10.1177/1474885111430616.

Schmitt, C. (1988) *Crisis of Parliamentary Democracy.* Later Printing Used edition. Translated by E. Kennedy. Cambridge, MA: The MIT Press.

Schrödinger, E. (1951) *What is Life?: The Physical Aspect of the Living Cell: Based on Lectures Delivered Under the Auspices of the Institute at Trinity College, Dublin, in February 1943.* Cambridge, UK: Cambridge University Press.

Scott, J. (1999) *Seeing Like a State: How Certain Schemes to Improve the Human Condition Have Failed.* New edition. New Haven, CT: Yale University Press.

Selbst, A.D., Boyd, D., Friedler, S., Venkatasubramanian, S. and Vertesi, J. (2018) *Fairness and Abstraction in Sociotechnical Systems.* SSRN Scholarly Paper ID 3265913. Rochester, NY: Social Science Research Network. Available at: https://papers.ssrn.com/abstract=3265913 (Accessed: 6 December 2020).

Selwyn, R. (2018) 'Predictive Analytics - Supporting Families Programme'. Available at: https://supportingfamilies.blog.gov.uk/2018/05/14/predictive-analytics/ (Accessed: 20 February 2022).

Shane, S., Metz, C. and Wakabayashi, D. (2018) 'How a Pentagon Contract Became an Identity Crisis for Google (Published 2018)', *The New York Times*, 30 May. Available at: https://www.nytimes.com/2018/05/30/technology/google-project-maven-pentagon.html (Accessed: 21 December 2020).

Shapin, S. and Schaffer, S. (2011) *Leviathan and the Air-Pump: Hobbes, Boyle, and the Experimental Life.* Princeton, NJ: Princeton University Press.

Shaw, D. (2020) *Philosophy of Antifascism: Punching Nazis and Fighting White Supremacy.* Illustrated edition. Lanham, MD: Rowman & Littlefield.

Simonite, T. (2020) 'Google Offers to Help Others With the Tricky Ethics of AI', *Wired*, 28 August. Available at: https://www.wired.com/story/google-help-others-tricky-ethics-ai/ (Accessed: 28 December 2020).

Smith, A. (2014) *Socially Useful Production.* STEPS Working Paper 58. Available at: https://steps-centre.org/publication/socially-useful-production/ (Accessed: 5 July 2021).

Smith, R.E. (2019) *Rage Inside the Machine: The Prejudice of Algorithms, and How to Stop the Internet Making Bigots of Us All.* New York, NY: Bloomsbury Business.

Solon, O. (2021) 'Drought-Stricken Communities Push Back Against Data Centers', *NBC News*, 19 June. Available at: https://www.nbcnews.com/tech/internet/drought-stric ken-communities-push-back-against-data-centers-n1271344 (Accessed: 16 August 2021).

Spade, D. (2015) *Normal Life: Administrative Violence, Critical Trans Politics, and the Limits of Law*. Durham, NC; London, UK: Duke University Press.

Spivak, G.C. (1988) *Can the Subaltern Speak?* Basingstoke, UK: Macmillan.

Stanley, J. (2021) 'Four Problems with the ShotSpotter Gunshot Detection System', *American Civil Liberties Union*, 24 August. Available at: https://www.aclu.org/news/privacy-technology/ four-problems-with-the-shotspotter-gunshot-detection-sys tem/ (Accessed: 7 November 2021).

Statewatch (2020) 'EU: Police Seeking New Technologies as Europol's "Innovation Lab" Takes Shape', *Statewatch*, 18 November. Available at: https://www.statewatch.org/news/ 2020/november/eu-police-seeking-new-technologies-as-euro pol-s-innovation-lab-takes-shape/ (Accessed: 11 December 2020).

Steyn, J. (2004) 'Guantanamo Bay: The Legal Black Hole', *International & Comparative Law Quarterly*, 53(1), pp 1–15. doi:10.1093/iclq/53.1.1.

Stop LAPD Spying Coalition (2020) 'Open Letter: Reject LAPD Face Recognition', *Knock LA*, 14 December. Available at: https://knock-la.com/open-letter-reject-lapd-face-recognit ion-e970e5ad68b3/ (Accessed: 31 October 2021).

Streitfeld, D. (2016) '"I'm Here to Help," Trump Tells Tech Executives at Meeting', *The New York Times*, 14 December. Available at: https://www.nytimes.com/2016/12/14/technol ogy/trump-tech-summit.html (Accessed: 24 January 2021).

Strubell, E., Ganesh, A. and McCallum, A. (2019) 'Energy and Policy Considerations for Deep Learning in NLP', *arXiv:1906.02243 [cs]* [Preprint]. Available at: http://arxiv. org/abs/1906.02243 (Accessed: 22 December 2020).

Szalavitz, M. (2021) 'The Pain Was Unbearable. So Why Did Doctors Turn Her Away?', *Wired*, 8 November. Available at: https://www.wired.com/story/opioid-drug-addiction- algorithm-chronic-pain/ (Accessed: 3 October 2021).

Tarnoff, B. (2020) 'The Making of the Tech Worker Movement', *Logic Magazine*, 4 May. Available at: https://logicmag.io/the-making-of-the-tech-worker-movement/full-text/ (Accessed: 21 December 2020).

Thatcher, M. (1987) 'Interview for Woman's Own ("No Such Thing as Society")', *Margaret Thatcher Foundation*, 31 October. Available at: https://www.margaretthatcher.org/document/106689 (Accessed: 11 December 2020).

The Intercept (2014) 'March 2013 Watchlisting Guidance', 23 July. Available at: https://theintercept.com/document/2014/07/23/march-2013-watchlisting-guidance/ (Accessed: 20 February 2022).

'The Lucas Plan' (2016). Available at: http://lucasplan.org.uk/ (Accessed: 22 January 2017).

The Partnership on AI (2016) Available at: https://www.partnershiponai.org/ (Accessed: 21 December 2020).

The UCL Institute of Health Equity (2020) 'Build Back Fairer: The COVID-19 Marmot Review', *Institute of Health Equity*, 15 December. Available at: http://www.instituteofhealthequity.org/about-our-work/latest-updates-from-the-institute/build-back-fairer (Accessed: 2 January 2021).

The Wiener Holocaust Library (2020) 'A Virtual Conversation: "Race Science" and Eugenics in Historical and Contemporary Context'. Available at: https://www.youtube.com/watch?v=f54_kk9ChIs (Accessed: 14 April 2021).

Thompson, E.P. (1993) *Customs in Common*. New edition. London, UK; New York, NY: Penguin Books Ltd.

Tidball, M. (2020) 'An Affront to Dignity, Inclusion and Equality: Coronavirus and the Impact of Law, Policy, Practice and Access to Services on People with Disabilities in the United Kingdom', *Oxford University Disability Law & Policy Project*, 2 July. Available at: https://www.law.ox.ac.uk/news/2020-07-02-affront-dignity-inclusion-and-equality-coronavirus-and-impact-law-policy-practice (Accessed: 15 December 2020).

Tilley, L. (2018) 'Populist Academics, Colonial Demography, and Far-Right Discursive Ecologies', *Discover Society*, 4 December. Available at: https://archive.discoversociety.org/2018/12/04/populist-academics-colonial-demography-and-far-right-discursive-ecologies/ (Accessed: 8 January 2021).

Tilley, L. (2020) 'Saying the Quiet Part Out Loud: Eugenics and the "Aging Population" in Conservative Pandemic Governance', *Discover Society*, 6 April. Available at: https://disc oversociety.org/2020/04/06/saying-the-quiet-part-out-loud-eugenics-and-the-aging-population-in-conservative-pande mic-governance/ (Accessed: 8 January 2021).

Towell, N. (2017) 'Parliamentary Committee Finds Centrelink Robo-Debt System Has Had "Profoundly Negative Impact"', *The Sydney Morning Herald*, 21 June. Available at: https:// www.smh.com.au/politics/federal/robodebt-has-harmed-thousands-say-senators-20170621-gwvgzg.html (Accessed: 7 December 2020).

Uber Engineering (2018) 'Uber Tech Day: What's My ETA? The Billion Dollar Question'. Available at: https://www.youtube.com/watch?v=FEebOd-Pdwg (Accessed: 11 January 2021).

UK Biobank (2018) Available at: http://www.nealelab.is/uk-biobank (Accessed: 9 December 2020).

van den Hoven, E. (2019) 'Automated Hermeneutical Injustice?', *COHUBICOL,* 16 August. Available at: https:// www.cohubicol.com/blog/automated-hermeneutical-injust ice/ (Accessed: 7 December 2020).

van Doorn, N. and Badger, A. (2020) 'Platform Capitalism's Hidden Abode: Producing Data Assets in the Gig Economy', *Antipode*, 52(5), pp 1475–95. doi:10.1111/anti.12641.

Veale, M. and Borgesius, F.Z. (2021) 'Demystifying the Draft EU Artificial Intelligence Act', *arXiv:2107.03721 [cs]* [Preprint]. Available at: http://arxiv.org/abs/2107.03721 (Accessed: 23 July 2021).

Vgontzas, N. (2021) 'Amazon After Bessemer', *Boston Review*, 21 April. Available at: https://bostonreview.net/class-inequal ity/nantina-vgontzas-amazon-after-bessemer (Accessed: 23 October 2021).

Vincent, J. (2021) 'Automatic Gender Recognition Tech Is Dangerous, Say Campaigners: It's Time to Ban It', *The Verge*, 14 April. Available at: https://www.theverge.com/ 2021/4/14/22381370/automatic-gender-recognition-sex ual-orientation-facial-ai-analysis-ban-campaign (Accessed: 10 November 2021).

Wade, B. (2018) 'This New Feminist Antifa Group Is Taking on the Far-Right', *Vice*, 15 October. Available at: https://www.vice.com/en/article/neg58q/feminist-antifascism-assembly-protest-london (Accessed: 4 September 2021).

Watkins, J., Wulaningsih, W., Da Zhou, C., Marshall, D.C., Sylianteng G.D.C., Dela Rosa, P.G., et al (2017) 'Effects of Health and Social Care Spending Constraints on Mortality in England: A Time Trend Analysis', *BMJ Open*, 7(11), p e017722. doi:10.1136/bmjopen-2017-017722.

Weber, M. (1978) *Economy and Society: An Outline of Interpretive Sociology*. New edition. Edited by G. Roth and C. Wittich. Berkeley, CA: University of California Press.

West, S.M., Whittaker, M. and Crawford, K. (2019) *Discriminating Systems: Gender, Race, and Power in AI*. AI Now Institute. Available at: https://ainowinstitute.org/discriminatingsystems.pdf

Whitehead, A.N. (1997) *Science and the Modern World*. New York, NY: Simon and Schuster.

Wills, T. (2019) 'Sweden: Rogue Algorithm Stops Welfare Payments for up to 70,000 Unemployed', *AlgorithmWatch*, 25 February. Available at: https://algorithmwatch.org/en/rogue-algorithm-in-sweden-stops-welfare-payments/ (Accessed: 7 December 2020).

Winner, L. (1988) *The Whale and the Reactor: A Search for Limits in an Age of High Technology*. New edition. Chicago, IL: University of Chicago Press.

Winnett, R. and Kirkup, J. (2012) 'Problem Families "Have Too Many Children"', *The Telegraph*, 20 July. Available at: https://www.telegraph.co.uk/news/politics/9416535/Problem-families-have-too-many-children.html (Accessed: 11 January 2021).

Witte, J.S. (2010) 'Genome-Wide Association Studies and Beyond', *Annual Review of Public Health*, 31(1), pp 9–20. doi:10.1146/annurev.publhealth.012809.103723.

Wolf, A. (2020) 'Robodebt Was an Algorithmic Weapon of Calculated Political Cruelty', *The Canberra Times*, 1 June. Available at: https://www.canberratimes.com.au/story/6775350/robodebt-was-an-algorithmic-weapon-of-calculated-political-cruelty/ (Accessed: 7 December 2020).

Wu, X. and Zhang, X. (2016) 'Automated Inference on Criminality using Face Images', *arXiv:1611.04135* [cs] [Preprint]. Available at: http://arxiv.org/abs/1611.04135 (Accessed: 11 December 2020).

Wynants, L., Van Calster, B., Collins, G.S., Riley R.D., Heinze, G., Schuit, E., et al (2020) 'Prediction Models for Diagnosis and Prognosis of Covid-19: Systematic Review and Critical Appraisal', *BMJ*, 369, p m1328. doi:10.1136/bmj.m1328.

Young, T. (2018) 'The Left is Heading for a Reckoning With the New Genetics', *The Spectator*, 23 April. Available at: https://www.spectator.co.uk/article/the-left-is-heading-for-a-reckoning-with-the-new-genetics (Accessed: 9 December 2020).

Youxuan, L. (2020) 'Takeaway Rider, Stuck in the System', 8 September. Available at: https://mp.weixin.qq.com/s/Mes1RqIOdp48CMw4pXTwXw (Accessed: 28 December 2021).

Index

Printed and bound by CPI Group (UK) Ltd, Croydon, CR0 4YY

16/04/2025

14658339-0002